15分钟外语随身学系列

15-MINUTE
CHINESE

GW00707714

15分钟外语随身学系列

15·MINUTE
CHINESE

每天15分钟学

汉 语

马骋 著

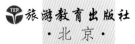

旅游教育出版社
·北京·

A Dorling Kindersley Book
www.dk.com

Original Title: Eyewitness Travel 15-Minute Chinese

Copyright © 2008 Dorling Kindersley Limited

图书在版编目（CIP）数据

每天15分钟学汉语=15-Minute Chinese /马骋
著. —北京：旅游教育出版社，2010.1
（15分钟外语随身学系列）
ISBN 978-7-5637-1923-5

I.①每… II.①马… III.①汉语—口语—对外
汉语教学–自学参考资料 IV.①H195.4

中国版本图书馆CIP数据核字（2009）第
234016号

15分钟外语随身学系列
每天15分钟学汉语
15-MINUTE CHINESE
马骋 著

责任编辑：郑凤

出版单位：旅游教育出版社
地　　址：北京市朝阳区定福庄南里1号
邮　　编：100024
发行电话：（010）65778403 65728372
　　　　　　　　65767462（传真）
本社网址：www.tepcb.com
E-mail：tepfx@163.com
印刷单位：中华商务联合印刷有限公司
经销单位：新华书店
开　　本：648×800　1/32
印　　张：5
字　　数：176千字
版　　次：2010年1月第1版
印　　次：2010年1月第1次印刷
印　　数：6000册
定　　价：29.80元（含光盘）

（图书如有装订差错请与发行部联系）

北京市版权局著作权合同登记图字：01–
2009–7573

Contents

How to use this book　　　6

Week 1
Introductions

Hello　　　8
My family　　　10
Your relatives　　　12
To be/to have　　　14
Review and repeat　　　16

Week 2
Eating and drinking

In the café　　　18
In the restaurant　　　20
Dishes　　　22
Requests　　　24
Review and repeat　　　26

Week 3
Making arrangements

Days and months　　　28
Time and numbers　　　30
Appointments　　　32
On the telephone　　　34
Review and repeat　　　36

Week 4
Travel

At the train station　　　38
To go/to take　　　40
Bus, taxi, and underground　　　42
On the road　　　44
Review and repeat　　　46

Week 5
Getting about

About town	48
Asking for directions	50
Sightseeing	52
At the airport	54
Review and repeat	56

Week 6
Accommodation

Booking a room	58
In the hotel	60
Hot spas	62
Adjectives	64
Review and repeat	66

Week 7
Shopping

Department store	68
Electronics store	70
At the supermarket	72
Clothes and shoes	74
Review and repeat	76

Week 8
Work and study

Jobs	78
The office	80
At the conference	82
In business	84
Review and repeat	86

Week 9
Health

At the chemist	88
The body	90
With the doctor	92
In hospital	94
Review and repeat	96

Week 10
At home

Home	98
Inside the home	100
The garden	102
Animals	104
Review and repeat	106

Week 11
Services

Post office and bank	108
Repairs	110
To come	112
Police and crime	114
Review and repeat	116

Week 12
Leisure and socializing

Leisure time	118
Sport and hobbies	120
Socializing	122
Review and repeat	124

Reinforce and progress	126
Menu guide	128
Dictionary	138
The Chinese writing system	152
Useful signs	158
Acknowledgments	160

How to use this book

The main part of the book is devoted to 12 themed chapters, broken down into five 15-minute daily lessons, the last of which is a revision lesson. So, in just 12 weeks you will have completed the course. A concluding reference section contains a menu guide, an English-to-Chinese dictionary, and a guide to Chinese characters.

Warm up and clock
Each day starts with a 1-minute warm up that encourages you to recall vocabulary or phrases you have learned previously. A clock to the right of the heading bar indicates the amount of time you are expected to spend on each exercise.

Useful phrases
Selected phrases relevant to the topic help you speak and understand.

Cultural/Conversational tip
These panels provide additional insights into life in China and language usage.

Text styles
Chinese script and pinyin pronunciation (see box opposite) are included, as well as English translation.

In conversation
Illustrated dialogues reflecting how vocabulary and phrases are used in everyday situations appear throughout the book.

How to use the flap
The book's cover flaps allow you to conceal the Chinese so that you can test whether you have remembered correctly.

Review and repeat
A recap of selected elements of previous lessons helps to reinforce your knowledge.

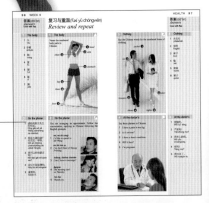

Instructions
Each exercise is numbered and introduced by instructions. In some cases, more information is given about the language point being covered.

LEISURE AND SOCIALIZING 123

Read it You now know the principle of how the Chinese script works and can recognize some basic recurring characters. You'll also find more information on pp.152–157 to help expand your understanding.

Put into practice

Join in this conversation.

Read it
These panels explain how the Chinese script works, show useful signs, and give tips for deciphering Chinese characters.

Read it
Chinese takes basic concepts and combines them to make different meanings, e.g. 飞机 feiji "plane" ("flying" fei + "machine" 机 ji); 火车 huoche "train" ("fire" 火 huo + "vehicle" 车 che).

Menu guide
Identify popular Chinese dishes on the menu with this guide.

Pinyin pronunciation guide

The Chinese taught in this book is Mandarin Chinese, the main language of the People's Republic of China (PRC). The pronunciation is written in pinyin, the official romanization system used in PRC schools. Most pinyin spellings reflect the nearest equivalent sound in English, but some letters sound different:

a pinyin **x** is pronounced like "sh" as in "ship"
a pinyin **c** is pronounced like "ts" as in "sits"
a pinyin **z** is pronounced like "ds" as in "kids"
a pinyin **q** is pronounced like "ch" as in "chin"
a pinyin **zh** is pronounced like "j" as in "just"
a pinyin **ü** is an "u" pronounced with rounded lips, like "few" in English or "über" in German

Mandarin Chinese has four "tones", which affect the way a word is pronounced. Each syllable is pronounced with one of four tones: high, rising, falling–rising, and falling. These tones can be written as accents on the pinyin pronunciation, but you need to listen to and mimic native speakers to master them. Use the *15-Minute Chinese* audio CD to practise your pronunciation, and the written pinyin as a memory aid.

Say it
In these exercises you are asked to apply the vocabulary you have learned in different contexts.

5 Say it

Do you have any single rooms?

Two nights.

Is dinner included?

Dictionary
A mini-dictionary provides ready reference from English to Chinese for 2,500 words.

138 DICTIONARY

Dictionary
English to Chinese

This dictionary contains the vocabulary from *15-Minute Chinese*, together with many other high-frequency words. You can also find additional terms for food and drink in the Menu Guide (pp.128–137). In Chinese, the plural of nouns is normally the same as the singular. Chinese descriptive words, or adjectives, may have different endings depending on how they are used and are also often preceded by *hen* ("very"). Verbs have no tenses and don't generally change according to who or what is the subject, but there are some characters that can be added to indicate a particular time or mood—see p.112.

128 MENU GUIDE

Menu guide

The guide lists the most common terms you may encounter on Chinese menus. Dishes are divided into categories and the Chinese script is displayed clearly to help you identify items on a menu.

Rice and noodle dishes

miàntiáo	面条	noodles
mǐfàn	米饭	rice
nuòmǐ	糯米	glutinous rice
chǎofàn	炒饭	fried rice
dàn chǎofàn	蛋炒饭	fried rice with egg
chǎomiàn	炒面	fried noodles
chǎo mǐfàn	炒米粉	fried rice noodles
zhōu	粥	rice porridge

Basic food items

chūnjuǎn	春卷	spring rolls
dòushābāo	豆沙包	steamed dumplings with sweet bean paste filling
huājuǎn	花卷	

1 Warm up

The Warm up panel appears at the beginning of each topic. Use it to reinforce what you have already learned and to prepare yourself for moving ahead with the new subject.

你好(nǐhǎo)
Hello

Chinese *gongshou* is famous: cupping one hand in the other in front of the chest, which is often accompanied with nodding or a slight bow. Traditionally, there would not be any contact in the form of a handshake or kisses, although this is changing with the increasing Western influence.

2 Words to remember

Say these expressions aloud. Hide the text on the left with the cover flap and try to remember the Chinese for each. Check your answers.

你好。
Nǐhǎo.
Hello!

早上好。 Zǎoshang hǎo.	*Good morning.*
晚上好。 Wǎnshang hǎo.	*Good evening.*
我的名字是…… Wǒ de míngzi shì...	*My name is...*
很高兴认识你。 Hěn gāoxìng rènshi nǐ.	*Pleased to meet you.*
再见。 Zàijiàn.	*Goodbye.*
晚安。 Wǎn'ān.	*Good night.*
明天见。 Míngtiān jiàn.	*See you tomorrow.*

3 In conversation: formal

你好，我的名字是韩红。
Nǐhǎo, wǒ de míngzi shì Hán Hóng.

Hello. My name is Han Hong.

你好，我的名字是罗伯特·巴克尔。
Nǐhǎo, wǒ de míngzi shì Luóbótè Bākè'ěr.

Hello. My name is Robert Barker.

很高兴认识你。
Hěn gāoxìng rènshi nǐ.

Pleased to meet you.

4 Put into practice

Join in this conversation. Read the Chinese beside the pictures on the left and then follow the instructions to make your reply. Test yourself by concealing the answers with the cover flap.

晚上好。
Wǎnshang hǎo.
Good evening.

Say: *Good evening.*

晚上好。
Wǎnshang hǎo.

我的名字是严峻盟。
Wǒ de míngzi shì Yán Jùnméng.
My name is Yan Junmeng.

Say: *Pleased to meet you.*

很高兴认识你。
Hěn gāoxìng rènshi nǐ.

Conversational tip The Chinese usually introduce themselves using either just the family name—Han—or the family name followed by the given name—Han Hong. But they are used to hearing Western names the other way: Robert Barker. It's not common to ask someone their name directly, so listen carefully to the introductions. When talking to or about others in an informal situation, "Xiao" or "Lao" is often added in front of their family name depending on whether they are perceived to be younger or older than you. For example, if Han Hong appears younger or more junior, you'd call her/him "Xiao Han"; if older or more senior, "Lao Han" is used to show respect.

5 In conversation: informal

明天见。
Míngtiān jiàn.

See you tomorrow.

好，明天见。
Hǎo, míngtiān jiàn.

Yes, see you tomorrow.

再见。
Zàijiàn.

Goodbye.

1 Warm up

Say "hello" and "goodbye" in Chinese. (pp.8–9)

Now say "My name is…". (pp.8–9)

Say "Pleased to meet you". (pp.8–9)

我的家庭(wǒ de jiātíng)
My family

Chinese has two sets of vocabulary for many family members, depending on whether you are talking about your own or someone else's. This lesson focusses on speaking about your own family. There's often no need for a separate word meaning *my*: **baba** means <u>*my father*</u>, **gege** <u>*my*</u> *big brother*, etc.

2 Match and repeat

Look at the numbered family members in this scene and match them with the vocabulary list at the side. Read the Chinese words aloud. Now, hide the list with the cover flap and test yourself.

1 奶奶
   nǎinai

2 爷爷
   yéye

3 爸爸
   bàba

4 妈妈
   māma

5 儿子
   érzi

6 女儿
   nǚ'ér

❶ *my grandmother*

❷ *my grandfather*

❸ *my father*

❹ *my mother*

❺ *my son*

❻ *my daughter*

Conversational tip Chinese distinguishes between "little" and "big" sister or brother. You will find all the relevant words in section 4. The phrase "xiongdi jiemei" (siblings) is used to refer to your brothers and sisters as a group: "wo you si ge xiongdi jiemei" (I have four siblings).

Words to remember: numbers

Memorize these words and then test yourself using the cover flap.

The Chinese use a system of "classifiers" to count specific things. These vary with the nature of what is being counted. The numbers opposite use the near universal classifier 个 **ge**. You can use this classifier when talking about your family, but it's useful to recognize another classifier 人 **ren** used for people. (Note the alternative character 二 **er** used for the number "two").

one	一个	yī gè
two	两个	liǎng gè
three	三个	sān gè
four	四个	sì gè
five	五个	wǔ gè
six	六个	liù gè
seven	七个	qī gè
eight	八个	bā gè
nine	九个	jiǔ gè
ten	十个	shí gè
eleven	十一个	shíyī gè
twelve	十二个	shí'èr gè

一人 yī rén   1 person
二人 èr rén   2 people
三人 sān rén   3 people
四人 sì rén   4 people
五人 wǔ rén   5 people
六人 liù rén   6 people
七人 qī rén   7 people
八人 bā rén   8 people
九人 jiǔ rén   9 people
十人 shí rén   10 people

Words to remember: relatives

Look at these words and say them aloud. Hide the text on the right with the cover flap and try to remember the Chinese. Check your answers and repeat, if necessary. Then practise the phrases below.

妻
qī
my wife

夫
fū
my husband

我们是夫妻。
Wǒmen shì fūqī.
We're married. ("We're husband and wife.")

my big sister/ my little sister	姐姐/妹妹	jiějie/mèimei
my big brother/ my little brother	哥哥/弟弟	gēge/ dìdi
my siblings	兄弟姐妹	xiōngdì jiěmèi
This is my wife.	这是我的妻子。	Zhè shì wǒ de qīzi.
I have four children.	我有四个孩子。	Wǒ yǒu sì gè háizi.
We have three daughters.	我有三个女儿。	Wǒ yǒu sān gè nǚ'ér.

你的家庭(nǐ de jiātíng)
Your relatives

1 Warm up

Say the Chinese for as
many members of
(your own) family as
you can. (pp.10–11)

Say "I have two sons."
(pp.10–11)

Chinese pronouns are straightforward:
I or *me* is **wo**, *you* is **ni** (or the more formal
nin), and *he/she* or *him/her* is **ta**. The plural
equivalents are made by adding **men**: *we*
women, *you* (plural) **nimen**, *they* **tamen**; and the
possessives by adding **de**: *my/mine* **wo de**,
your/yours **ni de**, *their/theirs* **tamen de**, etc.

2 Words to remember

Here are the more respectful terms used to refer to someone else's family, or
sometimes to your own in more formal situations.

母亲 mǔqin	*mother*
父亲 fùqin	*father*
儿子 érzi	*son*
女儿 nǚ'ér	*daughter*
妻子 qīzi	*wife*
丈夫 zhàngfu	*husband*
孩子 háizi	*children*
兄弟姐妹 xiōngdì jiěmèi	*siblings*

这是你的母亲吗?
Zhè shì nǐ de mǔqin ma?

Is this your mother?

3 In conversation

这是你的丈夫吗?
Zhè shì nǐ de zhàngfu
ma?

Is this your husband?

是的。这是我的父亲。
Shì de. Zhè shì wǒ de
fùqin.

*That's right. And this is
my father.*

你有孩子吗?
Nǐ yǒu háizi ma?

*Do you have any
children?*

Conversational tip Forming a question in Chinese is straightforward. Generally, you add the question marker "ma" (吗) to the end of a sentence. "na shi ni de erzi" (That's your son); "na shi ni de erzi ma?" (Is that your son?). In very informal spoken Chinese, the question marker is sometimes even dropped "na shi ni de erzi?"

4 Useful phrases

Read these phrases aloud several times and try to memorize them. Conceal the Chinese with the cover flap and test yourself.

Do you have any siblings? (formal)	您有兄弟姐妹吗? Nín yǒu xiōngdì jiěmèi ma?
Do you have any siblings? (informal)	你有兄弟姐妹吗? Nǐ yǒu xiōngdì jiěmèi ma?

Is this your father?	这是你爸爸吗? Zhè shì nǐ bàba ma?
Is that your son? (formal)	那是您的儿子吗? Nà shì nín de érzi ma?

This is Han Hong's daughter.	这是韩红的女儿。 Zhè shì Hán Hóng de nǚ'ér.
Is that your little sister? (informal)	那是你妹妹吗? Nà shì nǐ mèimei ma?

没有。但我有一个妹妹。
Méiyǒu. Dàn wǒ yǒu yī gè mèimei.

No, but I have a little sister.

5 Say it

Is this your wife?

Is that your little brother?

Do you have a son? (informal)

This is Han Hong's mother.

1 Warm up

Say "See you tomorrow." (pp.8–9)

Say "We're married" (pp.10–11) and "Is this your wife?" (pp.12–13)

是/有 (shì/yǒu)
To be/to have

The most common verb in Chinese is **shi**, meaning *is*, *are*, or *am*. The i is pronounced only slightly, often making the word sound more like **shuh**. Shi does not change with the subject (*I, he, we*, etc.): **wo shi Luobote** (*I'm Robert*), **ta shi yisheng** (*He/she is a doctor*), **women shi Zhongguo ren** (*We're Chinese*).

2 Useful phrases with shi

Notice that nationalities are expressed by using the name of the country followed by 人 **ren** (*person/people*): **Zhongguoren** *Chinese* (literally *"China land person/people"*), **Meiguoren** *American* (*"America land person/people"*).

我是中国人。 Wǒ shì Zhōngguórén.	*I'm Chinese.*	
现在是10点钟。 Xiànzài shì shí diǎnzhōng.	*It's ten o'clock.*	
你是医生吗? Nǐ shì yīshēng ma?	*Are you a doctor?*	
韩红是学生。 Hán Hóng shì xuéshēng.	*Han Hong is a student.*	

Read it It's not as difficult to begin deciphering the Chinese script as it may appear. 15-Minute Chinese shows "simplified" characters as used in mainland China. These characters consist of a number of strokes ranging from one to more than twenty (一、二、三、四; one, two, three, four, etc.), similar to how an English word is made up of a number of letters. Some basic concepts are represented by a single character, e.g. 我 wo ("I/me"), 人 ren ("person"), and these are the common characters you can learn to recognize first. Many other concepts are represented by a combination of characters, e.g. 英国人 Yingguoren ("ying-land person", i.e. "English"). You'll find more details on pp.152–159.

我是英国人。
Wǒ shì Yīngguórén.
I'm English.

3 Useful phrases: talking about what you have

An informal and straightforward way to talk about possession is to use the expression 有 **you**, meaning *have* or *has*. Learn these phrases and then test yourself by concealing the answers with the cover flap.

I have three children.	我有三个孩子。 Wǒ yǒu sān gè háizi.
My son has a car.	我的儿子有车。 Wǒ de érzi yǒu chē.
I have a little sister.	我有一个妹妹。 Wǒ yǒu yī gè mèimei.
Do you have any children?	你有孩子吗？ Nǐ yǒu háizi ma?

你有名片吗?
Nǐ yǒu míngpiàn ma?
Do you have a business card?

4 Negatives

There are two principal ways to make a negative sentence in Chinese: by using the negative markers 不 **bu** or 没 **mei** in front of a verb. **bu** is often used with **shi**, and **mei** with **you**.

We're not American.	我们不是美国人。 Wǒmen bù shì Měiguórén.

I don't have a car.	我没有车。 Wǒ méiyǒu chē.

5 Put into practice

Join in this conversation. Read the Chinese beside the pictures on the left and then follow the instructions to make your reply. Then test yourself by concealing the answers with the cover flap.

晚上好。 Wǎnshang hǎo. *Good evening.*	晚上好, 我是罗伯特。 Wǎnshang hǎo, wǒ shì Luóbótè.

Say: Good evening. I'm Robert.

很高兴认识你。 Hěn gāoxìng rènshi nǐ. *Pleased to meet you.*	你有名片吗? Nǐ yǒu míngpiàn ma?

Ask: Do you have a business card?

答案(dá'àn)
Answers
Cover with flap

复习与重温(fùxí yǔ chóngwēn)
Review and repeat

1 How many?

1 三
  sān

2 九
  jiǔ

3 四
  sì

4 二
  èr

5 八
  bā

6 十
  shí

7 五
  wǔ

8 七
  qī

9 六
  liù

1 How many?

Hide the answers with the cover flap. Then say these Chinese numbers aloud. Check that you have remembered the Chinese correctly.

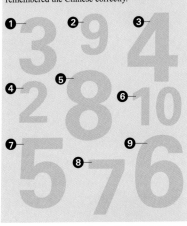

2 Hello

1 你好，我的名字
  是……
  Nǐhǎo, wǒ de
  míngzi shì...

2 很高兴认识你。
  Hěn gāoxìng
  rènshi nǐ.

3 我有三个儿子。
  你有孩子吗?
  Wǒ yǒu sān gè
  érzi. Nǐ yǒu háizi
  ma?

4 再见。
  Zàijiàn.

2 Hello

You meet someone in a formal situation. Join in the conversation, replying in Chinese following the English prompts.

nihao, wo de mingzi shi Yan Junmeng
1 *Answer the greeting and give your name.*

zhe shi wo de qizi
2 *Say "Pleased to meet you."*

ni you haizi ma
3 *Say "I have three sons.
   Do you have any children?"*

meiyou. dan wo you yi ge didi
4 *Say "Goodbye."*

答案(dá'àn)
Answers
Cover with flap

3 Be or have

Fill in the blanks with **shi** (*to be*) or **you** (*to have*). Then check your answers carefully.

1 wo _____ Zhongguoren

2 wo _____ san ge erzi

3 women _____ Yingguoren

4 Sarah _____ yisheng

5 ni _____ haizi ma

6 ta bu _____ xuesheng

7 wo de mingzi
_____ Han Hong

8 women mei _____ che

3 Be or have

1 是
shì

2 有
yǒu

3 是
shì

4 是
shì

5 有
yǒu

6 是
shì

7 是
shì

8 有
yǒu

4 Family

Say the Chinese for each of the numbered family members. Check your answers carefully.

❶ *my grandmother*

❷ *my grandfather*

my father ❸

❹ *my daughter*   ❻ *my mother*

❺ *my son*

4 Family

1 奶奶
nǎinai

2 爷爷
yéye

3 爸爸
bàba

4 女儿
nǚ'ér

5 儿子
érzi

6 妈妈
māma

1 Warm up

Count up to ten.
(pp.10–11)

Remind yourself how to
say "hello" and
"goodbye." (pp.8–9)

Ask "Do you have
any children?" (pp.14–15)

在咖啡厅(zài kāfēi tīng)
In the café

You will find different types of cafés
in China: there are traditional types, which
are called **chaguan**; and Western-style
coffee houses, simply called **kafei ting**.
These modern cafés are very popular,
particularly amongst young Chinese.

📷 **Cultural tip** The generic word for tea is "cha". Three
popular types are "lücha" (green tea—popular in eastern
China), "hongcha" (red tea—southern China), and "huacha"
(jasmine tea—northern China).

2 Words to remember

Look at the words below and say them out loud a
few times. Conceal the Chinese with the cover
flap and try to remember each one in turn. Also
practise the words on the right.

奶茶
nǎichá
tea with milk

绿茶 lǜchá	*green tea*
红茶 hóngchá	*red tea*
花茶 huāchá	*jasmine tea*
三明治 sānmíngzhì	*sandwich*

3 In conversation

请给我一杯咖啡。
Qǐng gěi wǒ yī bēi kāfēi.

I'd like a coffee.

还要其他食品吗?
Háiyào qítā shípǐn
ma?

Anything else?

有蛋糕吗?
Yǒu dàngāo ma?

*Do you have any
cakes?*

蛋糕
dàngāo
cake

Useful phrases

Learn these phrases. Read the English under the
pictures and say the phrase in Chinese as shown
on the right. Then cover up the answers on the
right and test yourself.

请给我一杯咖啡。
Qǐng gěi wǒ yī bēi kāfēi.

I'd like a coffee.

还要其他食品吗?
Háiyào qítā shípǐn ma?

Anything else?

糖
táng
sugar

还要一块蛋糕。
Háiyào yī kuài dàngāo.

A cake, too, please.

咖啡
kāfēi
coffee

多少钱?
Duōshao qián?

How much is that?

有,当然有。
Yǒu, dāngrán yǒu.

Yes, certainly.

还要一块蛋糕。
Háiyào yī kuài dàngāo.
多大钱?
Duōshao qián?

A cake, too, please.
How much is that?

50元……谢谢你。
Wǔshí yuán... xièxie nǐ.

*That's 50 yuan... thank
you.*

Warm up

Say "A coffee, please."
(pp.18–19)

Say "I don't have a
car." (pp.14–15)

Ask "Do you have any
cakes?" (pp.18–19)

在餐馆(zài cānguǎn)
In the restaurant

There are different types of eating places in China. You can find snacks or a light meal at street stalls. A **fanguan** serves traditional Chinese food. Department stores often house relaxed **canting** *(canteens)* on the upper floors, open until about 10pm and serving both international and Chinese dishes.

hand towel ❼

Words to remember

Familiarize yourself with these words and test yourself using the flap.

菜单 càidān	*menu*
酒水单 jiǔshuǐ dān	*wine list*
头盘 tóupán	*starters*
主食 zhǔshí	*main courses*
甜点 tiándiǎn	*desserts*
早餐 zǎocān	*breakfast*
午餐 wǔcān	*lunch*
晚餐 wǎncān	*dinner*

chopsticks ❻

❹ *fork*

❺ *spoon*

In conversation

请给我们安排一张四人餐桌。
Qǐng gěi wǒmen ānpái yī zhāng sì rén cānzhuō.

We'd like a table for four.

你们有预订吗?
Nǐmen yǒu yùdìng ma?

Do you have a reservation?

有。是巴克尔预订的。
Yǒu. Shì Bākè'ěr yùdìng de.

Yes, I do. In the name of Barker.

4 Match and repeat

Look at the numbered items in this table setting and match them with the Chinese words on the right. Read the Chinese words aloud. Now, conceal the Chinese with the cover flap and test yourself.

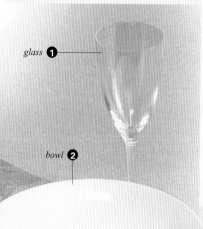

glass **1**

bowl **2**

plate **3**

1 酒杯
  jiǔbēi

2 碗
  wǎn

3 餐碟
  cāndié

4 叉子
  chāzi

5 调羹
  tiáogēng

6 筷子
  kuàizi

7 毛巾
  máojīn

5 Useful phrases

Practise these phrases and then test yourself using the cover flap to conceal the Chinese.

What type of noodles do you have?	你们供应哪些面条？ Nǐmen gōngyìng nǎxiē miàntiáo?
Where can I pay?	在哪儿付钱？ Zài nǎr fùqián?

你们想要吸烟区还是无烟区？
Nǐmen xiǎng yào xīyān qū háishì wúyān qū?

Would you like smoking or non-smoking?

我们想要无烟区。
Wǒmen xiǎng yào wúyān qū.

We'd like non-smoking.

好吧，这边请。
Hǎo ba, zhèbiān qǐng.

Very well. Here you are.

1 Warm up

Say "We're married" (pp.10–11) and "I'm English." (pp.14–15)

Ask "Do you have any siblings?" (pp.12–13)

Say "A sandwich, please." (pp.18–19)

菜肴(càiyáo)
Dishes

A typical meal in China consists of rice and a soup, together with a variety of fish, meat, and vegetable dishes. The meal is served with pickles and other condiments such as raw spring onions and chilli sauce depending on the region. Alcohol is consumed before the rice or noodles are served.

Cultural tip "Taocan" (set menus) are popular, particularly at lunchtime. These consist of a soup, rice, pickles, and other dishes—all presented on a tray. "Gaijiaofan" (rice with toppings) are a simpler alternative.

2 Match and repeat

Look at the numbered items and match them to the Chinese words in the panel on the left.

1 水果
shuǐguǒ

2 蔬菜
shūcài

3 面条
miàntiáo

4 海鲜
hǎixiān

5 汤
tāng

6 肉
ròu

7 鱼
yú

8 蘑菇
mógu

9 米饭
mǐfàn

1 *fruit*

8 *mushrooms*

9 *rice*

5 *soup*

7 *fish*

6 *meat*

Words to remember: cooking methods

Familiarize yourself with these words.

你们供应哪些肉？
Nǐmen gōngyìng nǎxiē ròu?
What type of meat do you have?

fried	炒	chǎo
grilled	烧	shāo
roasted	烤	kǎo
boiled	煮	zhǔ
steamed	蒸	zhēng
raw	生吃	shēng chī

Say it

What's "Nuomi"?

I'd like a baijiu.

What type of fish do you have?

Words to remember: drinks

Familiarize yourself with these words.

water	水	shuǐ
mineral water	矿泉水	kuàngquánshuǐ
"baijiu" (Chinese liquor/spirit)	白酒	báijiǔ
wine	葡萄酒	pútáojiǔ
beer	啤酒	píjiǔ
fruit juice	果汁	guǒzhī

vegetables

noodles

seafood

Useful phrases

Practise these phrases and then test yourself.

I'd like a beer.	请给我一杯啤酒。	Qǐng gěi wǒ yī bēi píjiǔ.
I'm vegetarian.	我是素食者。	Wǒ shì sùshízhě.
I'm allergic to nuts.	我对坚果过敏。	Wǒ duì jiānguǒ guòmǐn.
What's "Qianzhang"?	什么是千张？	Shénme shì qiānzhāng?

What are "breakfast", "lunch", and "dinner" in Chinese? (pp.20–21)

Say "I'm vegetarian" and "I'd like a fruit juice" in Chinese. (pp.22–23)

请求(qǐngqiú)

Requests

You've learned two common phrases that are used for asking for something: qing gei wo… *(I'd like…)* and qing gei women… *(We'd like…).* Alternatively, you can say what you want followed by hao ma *(please)*: wo yao… hao ma *(I want…, please).* You can use this phrase in almost any situation.

2 Basic requests

Here are some phrases for making basic requests in Chinese using qing gei wo/gei women… and wo yao… hao ma. Learn these phrases and then test yourself by using the cover flap.

我要一个蛋糕，好吗？ Wǒ yào yī gè dàngāo, hǎo ma?	*I want a cake, please.*
我要一个叉子，好吗？ Wǒ yào yī gè chāzi, hǎo ma?	*I want a fork, please.*
请给我一杯茶。 Qǐng gěi wǒ yī bēi chá.	*I'd like a tea.*
请给我们安排一张 三人餐桌。 Qǐng gěi wǒmen ānpái yī zhāng sān rén cānzhuō.	*We'd like a table for three.*
请给我菜单。 Qǐng gěi wǒ càidān.	*I'd like the menu.*
我要一点糖果，好 吗？ Wǒ yào yīdiǎn tángguǒ, hǎo ma?	*I want some sweets, please.*
给我加满，好吗？ Gěi wǒ jiāmǎn, hǎo ma?	*Fill it up, please.* ("A full tank, please.")

请给我接王先生的
电话。
Qǐng gěi wǒ jiē Wáng
xiānsheng de diànhuà.
*I'd like to speak to
Mr Wang.*

Read it Some Chinese characters are simple and resemble the item they describe, such as the character for "people": 人 (ren). The PRC simplified the characters, although traditional versions are still used in some of the Chinese-speaking areas. The sign on the left is simplified characters, which say tingzhi yingye meaning "business stopped", or "closed".

3 Polite requests

In a business situation, you may want to appear ultra-polite by using the polite version of "you"—nín instead of nǐ—especially if talking to someone senior. Learn these phrases and then test yourself.

Would you please help me?

请您帮帮我，好吗?
Qǐng nín bāngbāng wǒ, hǎo ma?

Could I have your signature here, please?

请您在这里签名，好吗?
Qǐng nín zài zhèlǐ qiānmíng, hǎo ma?

Could I have your phone number, please?

请把您的电话号码给我，好吗?
Qǐng bǎ nín de diànhuà hàomǎ gěi wǒ, hǎo ma?

4 Put into practice

Join in this conversation. Read the Chinese beside the pictures on the left and then follow the instructions to make your reply in Chinese. Test yourself by hiding the answers with the cover flap.

晚上好。你们有预订吗?
Wǎnshang hǎo. Nǐmen yǒu yùdìng ma?
Good evening. Do you have a reservation?

Say: No. We'd like a table for three.

没有。请给我们安排一张三人餐桌。
Méi yǒu. Qǐng gěi wǒmen ānpái yì zhāng sān rén cānzhuō.

您想喝什么饮料?
Nín xiǎng hē shénme yǐnliào?
What would you like to drink?

Say: I'd like a beer.

请给我一杯啤酒。
Qǐng gěi wǒ yì bēi píjiǔ.

答案(dá'àn)
Answers
Cover with flap

复习与重温(fùxí yǔ chóngwēn)
Review and repeat

1 What food?

1 汤
tāng

2 蔬菜
shūcài

3 鱼
yú

4 肉
ròu

5 酒杯
jiǔbēi

6 米饭
mǐfàn

1 What food?

Name the numbered items.

❶ soup

❷ vegetables

❸ fish

❹ meat

glass ❺

2 This is my...

1 这是我的丈夫。
Zhè shì wǒ de
zhàngfu.

2 这是我的女儿。
Zhè shì wǒ de
nǚ'ér.

3 他们是我的兄弟
姐妹。
Tāmen shì wǒ de
xiōngdì jiěmèi.

2 This is my...

Say these phrases in Chinese.

1 *This is my husband.*

2 *This is my daughter.*

3 *These are my
siblings.*

3 I'd like...

1 请给我一个蛋糕。
Qǐng gěi wǒ yī gè
dàngāo.

2 请给我一点糖。
Qǐng gěi wǒ yīdiǎn
táng.

3 请给我一杯咖啡。
Qǐng gěi wǒ yī bēi
kāfēi.

4 请给我一杯茶。
Qǐng gěi wǒ yī bēi
chá.

3 I'd like...

Say "I'd like" the following:

cake ❶

❹ tea

sugar ❷

coffee ❸

答案(dá'àn)
Answers
Cover with flap

6 *rice*

chopsticks **7**

8 *noodles*

beer **10**

9 *hand towel*

What food?

7 筷子
kuàizi

8 面条
miàntiáo

9 毛巾
máojīn

10 啤酒
píjiǔ

Restaurant

You arrive at a restaurant. Join in the conversation, replying in Chinese wherever you see the English prompts.

wanshang hao
1 Ask *"Do you have a table for three?"*

nimen you yuding ma
2 Say *"Yes, we do. In the name of Barker."*

nimen xiang yao xiyan qu haishi wuyan qu
3 Say *"We'd like non-smoking."*

hao ba. zhebian qing
4 Say *"We'd like the menu, please."*

haiyao qita shipin ma
5 Ask *"Do you have a wine list?"*

Restaurant

1 有三个人的桌子
吗?
Yǒu sān gè rén de
zhuōzi ma?

2 有。是巴克尔预
订的。
Yǒu. Shì Bākè'ěr
yùdìng de.

3 我们想要无烟区。
Wǒmen xiǎng yào
wúyān qū.

4 请给我们菜单,
好吗?
Qǐng gěi wǒmen
càidān, hǎo ma?

5 有酒水单
吗?
Yǒu jiǔshuǐ
dān ma?

1 Warm up

How do you say
"I have four children"?
(pp.10–11)

Now say "We're not
English" and "I don't
have a car." (pp.14–15)

What is Chinese
for "my mother"?
(pp.10–11)

星期与月份 (xīngqī yǔ yuèfèn)
Days and months

The most important holiday of the year is the one-week Chinese New Year, which usually happens in early February. Two other long holidays are October 1st (Chinese National Day), which also lasts five days, and May 1st (International Labour Day), which lasts three days. Christmas isn't generally celebrated.

2 Words to remember: days of the week

Familiarize yourself with these words and test yourself using the flap.

星期一 xīngqīyī	*Monday*
星期二 xīngqī'èr	*Tuesday*
星期三 xīngqīsān	*Wednesday*
星期四 xīngqīsì	*Thursday*
星期五 xīngqīwǔ	*Friday*
星期六 xīngqīliù	*Saturday*
星期日 xīngqīrì	*Sunday*
今天 jīntiān	*today*
明天 míngtiān	*tomorrow*
昨天 zuótiān	*yesterday*

明天见。
Míngtiān jiàn.
We meet tomorrow.

我今天有预订。
Wǒ jīntiān yǒu yùdìng.
I have a reservation for today.

3 Useful phrases: days

There is no Chinese equivalent of *on* or *in*, as in *on Tuesday, in February.*

会议不是星期二。
Huìyì bù shì xīngqī'èr.

The meeting isn't on Tuesday.

我星期日工作。
Wǒ xīngqīrì gōngzuò.

I work on Sundays.

4 Words to remember: months of the year

Chinese months are named simply "1 month", "2 month", etc.

我们的结婚纪念日在
七月。
Wǒmen de jiéhūn jìniànrì
zài qīyuè.
*Our anniversary is
in July.*

中国春节一般在二月。
Zhōngguó Chūn Jié yībān
zài èryuè.
*Chinese New Year is
usually in February.*

January	一月 yīyuè
February	二月 èryuè
March	三月 sānyuè
April	四月 sìyuè
May	五月 wǔyuè
June	六月 liùyuè
July	七月 qīyuè
August	八月 bāyuè
September	九月 jiǔyuè
October	十月 shíyuè
November	十一月 shíyīyuè
December	十二月 shí'èryuè
next month	下个月 xiàgèyuè
last month	上个月 shànggèyuè

5 Useful phrases: months

Learn these phrases and then test yourself using the cover flap.

*My children are on
holiday in August.*

我的孩子八月放假。
Wǒ de háizi bāyuè
fàngjià.

*My birthday is
in June.*

我的生日在六月。
Wǒ de shēngrì zài
liùyuè.

时间和数字 (shíjiān hé shùzì)
Time and numbers

1 Warm up

Count in Chinese from one to twelve.
(pp.10–11)

Say "Do you have a reservation?"
(pp.20–21)

Say "The meeting isn't on Wednesday."
(pp.28–29)

When telling the time in Chinese, the hour comes first, for example, **yidian** (*one o'clock*), **jiudian** (*nine o'clock*), etc., followed by the minutes: **wufen** (*five minutes*), **shifen** (*ten minutes*). **Ban** is "a half" (*30 minutes*), **yike** "a quarter" (*15 minutes*), and **sanke** "three-quarters" (*45 minutes*).

2 Words to remember: time

Memorize how to tell the time in Chinese.

1点 yī diǎn	*one o'clock*
1点5分 yī diǎn wǔ fēn	*five past one*
1点一刻 yī diǎn yīkè	*quarter past one*
1点半 yī diǎn bàn	*half past one*
1点20分 yī diǎn èrshí fēn	*twenty past one*
1点三刻 yī diǎn sānkè	*quarter to two* ("one and three-quarters")
2点差10分 liǎng diǎn chà shí fēn	*ten to two*

3 Useful phrases

Learn these phrases and then test yourself using the cover flap.

现在几点了? Xiànzài jǐ diǎn le?	*What time is it?*	
你几点想吃早餐? Nǐ jǐ diǎn xiǎng chī zǎocān?	*At what time do you want breakfast?*	
我有一个12点的预订。 Wǒ yǒu yī gè shí'èr diǎn de yùdìng.	*I have a reservation for twelve o'clock.*	

4 Words to remember: higher numbers

Chinese numbers are very logical. To count above ten, the individual numbers are simply added together. So 11 is shiyi *("ten-one")*, 15 is shiwu *("ten-five")*, etc. Be careful, though, to put the numbers the right way around: wushi is 50 *("five-ten")*, qishi is 70 *("seven-ten")*. Units are added directly after the tens: 68 is liushi ba; 25 is ershi wu, and so on.

Pay special attention to the number 10,000, which is wan or yiwan. A million is yibai wan *("one hundred-ten thousands")*.

这是五百元。
Zhè shì wǔbǎi yuán.
That's 500 yuan.

eleven	十一	shíyī
twelve	十二	shí'èr
thirteen	十三	shísān
fourteen	十四	shísì
fifteen	十五	shíwǔ
sixteen	十六	shíliù
seventeen	十七	shíqī
eighteen	十八	shíbā
nineteen	十九	shíjiǔ
twenty	二十	èrshí
thirty	三十	sānshí
forty	四十	sìshí
fifty	五十	wǔshí
sixty	六十	liùshí
seventy	七十	qīshí
eighty	八十	bāshí
ninety	九十	jiǔshí
one hundred	一百	yībǎi
three hundred	三百	sānbǎi
one thousand	一千	yīqiān
ten thousand	一万	yīwàn
two hundred thousand	二十万	èrshí wàn
one million	一百万	yībǎi wàn

5 Say it

twenty-five

ninety-two

seven hundred

twenty thousand

five to ten

half past eleven

That's 75 yuan.

预约 (yùyuē)
Appointments

1 Warm up

Say the days of the week. (pp.28–29)

Say "three o'clock." (pp.30–31)

What is "today", "tomorrow", and "yesterday" in Chinese? (pp.28–29)

There's no fundamental difference when it comes to making an appointment and meeting someone for the first time. If it's a business meeting, people do exchange business cards first. When you do so, remember to hand over your business card with both hands.

2 Useful phrases

Learn these phrases and then test yourself.

我们明天见，好吗？ Wǒmen míngtiān jiàn, hǎo ma?	*Shall we meet tomorrow?*
和谁？ Hé shéi?	*With whom?*
您什么时候有空？ Nín shénme shíhou yǒu kòng?	*When are you free?*
对不起，那天我很忙。 Duìbuqǐ, nàtiān wǒ hěn máng.	*Sorry, I'm busy that day.*
星期四怎么样？ Xīngqīsì zěnmeyàng?	*How about Thursday?*
对我正合适。 Duì wǒ zhèng héshì.	*That's good for me.*

欢迎。
Huānyíng.
Welcome.

3 In conversation

你好，我有预约。
Nǐhǎo, wǒ yǒu yùyuē.

Hello. I have an appointment.

和谁？
Hé shéi?

With whom?

和王先生。
Hé Wáng xiānsheng.

With Mr Wang.

4 Put into practice

Practise these phrases. Then cover up the text on the right and say the answering part of the dialogue in Chinese. Check your answers and repeat if necessary.

我们星期四见面，好吗？
Wǒmen xīngqīsì jiànmiàn, hǎo ma?
Shall we meet on Thursday?

Say: Sorry, I'm busy that day.

对不起，那天我很忙。
Duìbuqǐ, nàtiān wǒ hěn máng.

您什么时候有空？
Nín shénme shíhou yǒu kòng?
When are you free?

Say: On Tuesday in the afternoon.

星期二下午我有空。
Xīngqī'èr xiàwǔ wǒ yǒu kòng.

对我正合适。
Duì wǒ zhèng héshì.
That's good for me.

Ask: At what time?

什么时间呢？
Shénme shíjiān ne?

Read it It's useful to recognize some common Chinese signs you might see around a building. The signs below are a combination of characters. The final character in each (处 chu) means "place" or "location".

接待处 jiēdài chù (reception)

问讯处 wènxùn chù (information desk)

很好。约的是什么时间？
Hěn hǎo. Yuē de shì shénme shíjiān?

Very good. What time is the appointment?

十点钟。
Shí diǎnzhōng.

At ten o'clock.

请坐吧。
Qǐng zuò ba.

Take a seat, please.

1 Warm up

How do you say "sorry"? (pp.32–33)

Ask "Shall we meet tomorrow?" (pp.32–33)

Say "I'd like a cake, please." (pp.24–25)

打电话 (dǎ diànhuà)
On the telephone

The Chinese usually answer the telephone with **wei** (*hello*), although sometimes **nihao** can also be used. You should not use **wei** for face-to-face greetings. Almost all public telephones have English instructions and work with phonecards (**dianhua ka** or **IP ka**) available at most stores.

2 Match and repeat

Match the numbered items to the Chinese in the panel on the left and test yourself.

1 充电器
chōngdiànqì

2 答录机
dálùjī

3 电话机
diànhuàjī

4 电话卡
diànhuàkǎ

5 手机
shǒujī

6 耳机
ěrjī

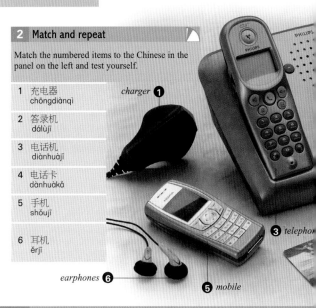

charger **1**

3 *telephone*

earphones **6**

5 *mobile*

3 In conversation

喂，我是总机。
Wèi, wǒ shì zǒngjī.

Hello, operator speaking. ("I am the operator.").

喂，请给我接王先生的电话。
Wèi, qǐng gěi wǒ jiē Wáng xiānsheng de diànhuà.

Hello, I'd like to speak to Mr Wang.

您是谁呀？
Nín shì shéi ya?

Who's calling?

4 Useful phrases

Practise these phrases. Then test yourself using the cover flap.

请给我接外线。
Qǐng gěi wǒ jiē wàixiàn.

I'd like an outside line.

我想买一张电话卡。
Wǒ xiǎng mǎi yī zhāng diànhuàkǎ.
I want to buy a phonecard, please.

请给我接王先生的电话。
Qǐng gěi wǒ jiē Wáng xiānsheng de diànhuà.

I'd like to speak to Mr Wang, please.

2 answering machine

我可以给他留言吗?
Wǒ kěyǐ gěi tā liúyán ma?

Can I leave a message?

对不起,我打错电话了。
Duìbuqǐ, wǒ dǎ cuò diànhuà le.

4 phonecard

Sorry, I have the wrong number.

我是大通印刷厂的张兴良。
Wǒ shì Dàtōng yìnshuā chǎng de Zhāng Xīngliáng.

I'm Zhang Xingliang from Tatong Printing.

对不起,电话占线。
Duìbuqǐ, diànhuà zhànxiàn.

I'm sorry, the line is busy.

可不可以让王先生给我回电话?
Kě bù kěyǐ ràng Wáng xiānsheng gěi wǒ huí diànhuà?

Can you ask Mr Wang to call me back?

复习与重温(fùxí yǔ chóngwēn)
Review and repeat

答案(dá'àn)
Answers
Cover with flap

1 Sums

1 十六
shíliù

2 三十九
sānshíjiǔ

3 五十三
wǔshísān

4 七十八
qīshíbā

5 九十九
jiǔshíjiǔ

6 十七
shíqī

1 Sums

Speak out loud the answers to these sums in Chinese. Then check your answers.

1 $10 + 6 = ?$

2 $14 + 25 = ?$

3 $66 - 13 = ?$

4 $40 + 38 = ?$

5 $90 + 9 = ?$

6 $20 - 3 = ?$

3 Telephones

What are the numbered items in Chinese?

mobile **1**

phonecard **3**

2 To want

1 请
qǐng

2 好
hǎo

3 茶
chá

4 给我
gěi wǒ

5 我
wǒ

6 电话
diànhuà

2 To want

Fill the gaps in these requests with the correct word.

1 _____ gei wo yi bei pijiu

2 wo yao yi ge dangao, _____ ma

3 qing gei wo yi bei nai_____

4 qing _____ jie waixian

5 _____ yao mai dianhua ka

6 qing gei wo jie Wang xiansheng de _____

答案(dá'àn)
Answers
Cover with flap

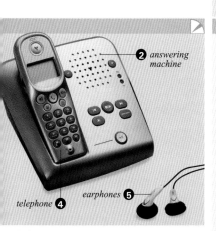

2 *answering machine*

telephone 4

earphones 5

3 Telephones

1 手机
shǒujī

2 答录机
dálùjī

3 电话卡
diànhuàkǎ

4 电话机
diànhuàjī

5 耳机
ěrjī

4 When?

What do these sentences mean?

1 mingtian jian

2 wo xingqiliu gongzuo

3 wo de shengri shi wuyue

4 wo jintian you yuding

4 When?

1 *We meet/see you tomorrow.*

2 *I work on Saturday.*

3 *My birthday is in May.*

4 *I have a reservation for today.*

5 Time

Say these times in Chinese.

5 Time

1 1点
yī diǎn

2 1点5分
yī diǎn wǔ fēn

3 1点20分
yī diǎn èrshí fēn

4 1点半
yī diǎn bàn

5 1点一刻
yī diǎn yīkè

6 2点差10分
liǎng diǎn chà shí fēn

1 Warm up

Count to 100 in tens. (pp.10–11 and pp.30–31)

Ask "What time is it?" (pp.30–31)

Say "half past one". (pp.30–31)

在火车站 (zài huǒchē zhàn)
At the train station

Each type of train service in China has a unique reference. This consists of an English letter followed by a number, which indicates the route and class. Generally, services beginning with D or Z are the fastest, non-stop trains, while K or T indicates express long-distance trains, stopping only at major stations.

2 Words to remember

Learn these words and then test yourself.

车站 chēzhàn	*station*
火车 huǒchē	*train*
站台 zhàntái	*platform*
车票 chēpiào	*ticket*
单程票 dānchéng piào	*single*
往返票 wǎngfǎn piào	*return*
硬卧车厢 yìngwò chēxiāng	*sleeper coach*
普通车厢 pǔtōng chēxiāng	*ordinary coach*

乘客 chéngkè *passenger*

出入口 chūrù kǒu *entry/exit*

车站很拥挤。 Chēzhàn hěn yōngjǐ. *The station is crowded.*

3 In conversation

我想买两张去北京的车票。 Wǒ xiǎng mǎi liǎngzhāng qù Běijīng de chēpiào.

Can I buy two tickets to Beijing, please?

往返票吗? Wǎngfǎn piào ma?

Is that return?

是的。我需要确定座位吗? Shì de. Wǒ xūyào quèdìng zuòwèi ma?

Yes. Do I need to make seat reservations?

4 Useful phrases

Learn these phrases and then test yourself using the cover flap.

How much is a ticket to Shanghai?	去上海的车票多少钱? Qù Shànghǎi de chēpiào duōshao qián?
Can I use a credit card?	可以用信用卡吗? Kěyǐ yòng xìnyòngkǎ ma?
Do I have to change?	需要换车吗? Xūyào huànchē ma?
Which platform does the train leave from?	从第几站台上车? Cóng dì-jǐ zhàntái shàngchē?
What time does the train leave?	火车几点发车? Huǒchē jǐ diǎn fāchē?

去上海的火车晚点了。
Qù shànghǎi de huǒchē wǎndiǎn le.
The train for Shanghai is late.

5 Say it

The train is crowded.

How much is a ticket to Beijing?

Cultural tip You can normally buy your rail tickets in advance from your hotel by paying a small handling fee. If this service is not available at your hotel, you can visit a travel agency or the station to buy tickets. You will need to pay in cash at the station. There are a few places where you can buy tickets from a machine.

不需要。总共100元。
Bù xūyào. Zǒnggòng yìbǎi yuán.

No. That's 100 yuan.

可以用信用卡吗?
Kěyǐ yòng xìnyòngkǎ ma?

Can I use a credit card?

我们只收现金。请从第一站台上车。
Wǒmen zhǐshōu xiànjīn. Qǐng cóng dì-yī zhàntái shàngchē.

We only take cash. The train leaves from platform one.

1 Warm up

How do you say "train"? (pp.38–39)

What are "tomorrow" and "yesterday" in Chinese? (pp.28–29)

Count from 10 to 20. (pp.30–31)

去/乘 (qù/chéng)
To go/to take

Qu (*to go*) and cheng (*to take*) are essential verbs you will need as you find your way around. Chinese verbs do not change according to the subject or tense as they do in English (*I go, you went*, etc.). A verb generally appears immediately after the subject, or "doer", of the action.

2 Qu/cheng: to go/to take

Read these phrases aloud several times and try to memorize them. Conceal the Chinese with the cover flap and test yourself.

你去哪儿? Nǐ qù nǎr?	*Where are you going?* *(informal)*
您要去哪儿? Nín yào qù nǎr?	*Where are you going?* *(formal)*
我去火车站。 Wǒ qù huǒchē zhàn.	*I'm going to the station.*
我乘地铁上班。 Wǒ chéng dìtiě shàngbān.	*I take the underground to work.*
我乘出租车上班。 Wǒ chéng chūzūchē shàngbān.	*I take a taxi to work.*
我要乘公共汽车去。 Wǒ yào chéng gōnggòng qìchē qù.	*I want to go by bus.*

今天我去长城。
Jīntiān wǒ qù Chángchéng.
Today I'm going to the Great Wall.

Cultural tip Taxis in China have signs clearly marked in both Chinese characters and English. Most of the major cities have ample taxis cruising the main streets and they are usually easy to hail. Otherwise, the hotel can order one. Fares are very reasonable by Western standards. Tipping is not customary, as it isn't in most service situations in China.

3 Past and future

The character 了 **le** or 过 **guo** immediately after a verb shows it is in the past: **qule** or **quguo** *(went/have been to)*. There is no special form for the future; the verb is used with a time indicator, e.g. **mingtian** *(tomorrow)*.

I took a taxi.

我乘了出租车。
Wǒ chéngle chūzūchē.

I went to the Great Wall.

我去了长城。
Wǒ qùle Chángchéng.

Tomorrow, I'll take the underground to work.

明天我乘地铁上班。
Míngtiān wǒ chéng dìtiě shàngbān.

Tomorrow, I'll take the bus to work.

明天我乘公共汽车上班。
Míngtiān wǒ chéng gōnggòng qìchē shàngbān.

4 Put into practice

Cover the text on the right and complete the dialogue in Chinese.

你去哪儿?
Nǐ qù nǎr?
Where are you going?

我去火车站。
Wǒ qù huǒchē zhàn.

Say: I'm going to the train station.

你要乘地铁吗?
Nǐ yào chéng dìtiě ma?
Do you want to take the underground?

不，我要乘公共汽车。
Bù, wǒ yào chéng gōnggòng qìchē.

Say: No, I want to take the bus.

你需要乘120路公共汽车。
Nǐ xūyào chéng yībǎi-èrshí lù gōnggòng qìchē.
That'll be bus number 120.

谢谢你。
Xièxie nǐ.

Say: Thank you.

1 Warm up

Say "I want to go
by bus." (pp.40–41)

Ask "Where are you
going?" (pp.40–41)

What's 88 in
Chinese? (pp.30–31)

公共汽车、出租车、地铁
(gōnggòng qìchē, chūzūchē, dìtiě)
Bus, taxi, and underground

On buses, you can generally buy your ticket from
a machine as you get on board. In smaller cities,
you can buy your tickets from a bus conductor.

2 Words to remember

Familiarize yourself with these words.

公共汽车/巴士 gōnggòng qìchē/bāshì	*bus*
出租车 chūzūchē	*taxi*
地铁 dìtiě	*underground*
公共汽车站 gōnggòng qìchē zhàn	*bus station*
出租车站 chūzūchē zhàn	*taxi rank*
地铁站 dìtiě zhàn	*underground station*
车票 chēpiào	*ticket*
路 lù	*line/route*

518路车在这儿停吗?
Wǔbǎi-yīshíbā lù chē zài
zhèr tíng ma?
*Does the number 518
stop here?*

3 In conversation: taxi

请带我去故宫, 好吗?
Qǐng dài wǒ qù Gùgōng,
hǎo ma?

*I'd like to go to the
Forbidden City, please.*

上车吧。
Shàngchē ba.

Do get in.

我就在这儿下车,
可以吗?
Wǒ jiù zài zhèr xiàchē,
kěyǐ ma?

*Can you drop me here,
please?*

4 Useful phrases

Learn these phrases and then test yourself using the cover flap.

I'd like a taxi to Dongdan, please.

请给我叫出租车去东单，好吗？
Qǐng gěi wǒ jiào chūzūchē qù Dōngdān, hǎo ma?

What time is the next bus to the airport?

下一趟去机场的巴士几点发车？
Xiàyītàng qù jīchǎng de bāshì jǐ diǎn fāchē?

How do you get to the Summer Palace?

去颐和园怎么走？
Qù Yíhéyuán zěnme zǒu?

Please wait for me.

请等等我。
Qǐng děngděng wǒ.

Cultural tip

Beijing and Shanghai have extensive metro systems. Station names can be recognized by a sign (as shown here), in both pinyin and Chinese. Fares are very reasonable.

6 Say it

I'd like to go to the Summer Palace, please.

I'd like a taxi to the Forbidden City.

How do you get to Dongdan?

5 In conversation: bus

这趟车去故宫博物院吗？
Zhè tàng chē qù Gùgōng Bówùyuàn ma?

Is this bus going to the Palace Museum?

是的。不很远。
Shì de. Bù hěn yuǎn.

Yes. It's not very far.

到了那里，您能告诉我吗？
Dàole nàli, nín néng gàosu wǒ ma?

Can you tell me when to get off?

1 Warm up

How do you say "I'd like a coffee, please"? (pp.14–15)

Say "my father", "my sister", and "my parents". (pp.12–13)

Say "I'm going to the Great Wall." (pp.40–41)

在路上 (zài lùshang)
On the road

There's a growing number of cars in Chinese cities and on the expressways. The road systems are expanding fast. Renting a car is not as unusual or difficult as it once was, although issues with licences and the crowded and unfamiliar roads make it preferable to also hire a driver.

2 Match and repeat

Match the numbered items to the list on the left, then test yourself.

1 挡风玻璃
dǎngfēng bōli

2 发动机盖
fādòngjīgài

3 保险杠
bǎoxiǎngàng

4 车胎
chētāi

5 前灯
qiándēng

6 车门
chēmén

7 车轮
chēlún

8 后舱
hòucāng

9 后视镜
hòushìjìng

Cultural tip Traffic in China moves on the right. The growing network of expressways is fast and efficient, but outside Beijing tolls are generally payable.

1 *windscreen*
2 *bonnet*
3 *bumper*
4 *tyre*
5 *headlights*

3 Road signs

单向行车道
dānxiàng xíngchē dào

One way traffic

出口
chūkǒu

Exit

最大时速
zuì dà shísù

Maximum speed

4 Useful phrases

Learn these phrases and then test yourself using the cover flap.

The engine won't start.
发动机无法启动。
Fādòngjī wúfǎ qǐdòng.

Fill it up, please.
请加满油箱。
Qǐng jiāmǎn yóuxiāng.

5 Words to remember

Familiarize yourself with these words then test yourself using the flap.

6 Say it

Oil, please.

The car won't start.

9 *wing mirror*

8 *boot*

6 *door*   **7** *wheel*

car	汽车 qìchē
driving licence	驾照 jiàzhào
petrol	汽油 qìyóu
oil	柴油 cháiyóu
engine	发动机 fādòngjī
flat tyre	车胎没气了 chētāi méiqì le

> ⁂ **Read it** Road signs are often written in Chinese characters only. If you're driving, familiarize yourself with the Chinese script for your destination, as well as the more common signs, such as 停 ting ("stop").

停
tíng

Stop

禁止进入
jìnzhǐ jìnrù

No entry

禁止停车
jìnzhǐ tíngchē

No parking

答案(dá'àn)
Answers
Cover with flap

复习与重温(fùxí yǔ chóngwēn)
Review and repeat

1 Transport

1 出租车
chūzūchē

2 自行车
zìxíngchē

3 汽车
qìchē

4 地铁
dìtiě

5 公共汽车
gōnggòng qìchē

1 Transport

Name these forms of transport
in Chinese.

1 *taxi*

bicycle **2**

5 *bus*

2 Go and take

1 去
qù

2 哪儿
nǎr

3 站
zhàn

4 上班
shàngbān

5 了/过
le/guò

6 乘
chéng

2 Go and take

Use the correct Chinese word to fill the gaps.

1 jintian wo _____ Changcheng

2 nin yao qu _____

3 wo qu huoche _____

4 wo cheng ditie qu _____

5 (zuotian) wo cheng_____ chuzuche

6 wo yao _____ gonggong qiche qu

答案(dá'àn)
Answers
Cover with flap

3 car

underground **4**

2 号线
LINE 2

3 ▸ Questions

How do you ask these questions in Chinese?

1 *"Do you have any cakes?"*

2 *"Do you have any children?"*

3 *"What time is it?"*

4 *"What time does the train leave?"*

5 *"Where are you going?"* *(informal).*

6 *"Can I use a credit card?"*

3 Questions

1 有蛋糕吗?
Yǒu dàngāo ma?

2 你有孩子吗?
Nǐ yǒu háizi ma?

3 现在几点了?
Xiànzài jǐ diǎn le?

4 火车几点发车?
Huǒchē jǐ diǎn fā-chē?

5 你去哪儿?
Nǐ qù nǎr?

6 可以用信用卡吗?
Kěyǐ yòng xìnyòngkǎ ma?

4 Tickets

You're buying tickets at a train station. Join in the conversation, replying in Chinese following the numbered English prompts.

zaoshang hao
1 *Can I buy two tickets to Shanghai, please?*

wangfan piao ma
2 *No. I want singles.*

zonggong yibai yuan
3 *What time does the train leave?*

liang dian cha shi fen
4 *Which platform does the train leave from?*

qing cong di-yi zhantai shangche
5 *Thank you.*

4 Tickets

1 我想买两张去上海的车票。
Wǒ xiǎng mǎi liǎng zhāng qù Shànghǎi de chēpiào.

2 不,我要单程票。
Bù, wǒ yào dānchéng piào.

3 火车几点发车。
Huǒchē jǐ diǎn fā-chē.

4 从第几站台上车?
Cóng dì-jǐ zhàntái shàngchē?

5 谢谢你。
Xièxie nǐ.

1 Warm up

Ask "Do you go to the museum?" (pp.42–43)

What are "station" and "ticket" in Chinese? (pp.38–39)

在城市内 (zài chéngshì nèi)
About town

To talk about features or facilities, you can use the word **you**. Earlier, we learned that **you** means *have/has*, but it can also mean *there is/are*. The opposite is **meiyou**. Notice the word order in Chinese: **daqiao fujin you youyongchi** = *bridge/near to/there is/ swimming pool* (*There's a swimming pool near the bridge*).

2 Match and repeat

Match the numbered locations to the words in the panel.

1 斑马线
  bānmǎxiàn

2 停车场
  tíngchēchǎng

3 喷泉
  pēnquán

4 百货大楼
  bǎihuò dàlóu

5 广场
  guǎngchǎng

6 博物馆
  bówùguǎn

7 电影院
  diànyǐngyuàn

8 大桥
  dàqiáo

❶ *crossing*

❷ *car park*

❸ *fountain*

❽ *bridge*

3 Words to remember

Familiarize yourself with these words and test yourself using the cover flap.

加油站 jiāyóuzhàn	*petrol station*
旅游服务中心 lǚyóu fúwù zhōngxīn	*tourist information centre*
游泳池 yóuyǒngchí	*swimming pool*
网吧 wǎngbā	*internet café*

❼ *cinema*

4 Useful phrases

Learn these phrases and then test yourself using the cover flap.

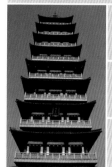

Is there a museum nearby?	附近有博物馆吗?	Fùjìn yǒu bówùguǎn ma?
Is it far from here?	离这里远吗?	Lí zhèlǐ yuǎn ma?
There's a swimming pool near the bridge.	大桥附近有游泳池。	Dàqiáo fùjìn yǒu yóuyǒngchí.
There isn't a tourist information centre.	没有旅游服务中心。	Méiyǒu lǚyóu fúwù zhōngxīn.

宝塔在市中心。
Bǎotǎ zài shì zhōngxīn.
The pagoda is in the centre of town.

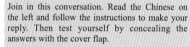

4 *department store*

5 Put into practice

Join in this conversation. Read the Chinese on the left and follow the instructions to make your reply. Then test yourself by concealing the answers with the cover flap.

没有问题吧?
Méiyǒu wèntí ba?
Is everything OK?

Ask: *Is there an internet café nearby?*

附近有网吧吗?
Fùjìn yǒu wǎngbā ma?

没有，但是有一个旅游服务中心。
Méiyǒu, dànshì yǒu yī gè lǚyóu fúwù zhōngxīn.
No there isn't, but there's a tourist information centre.

Ask: *Is it far from here?*

离这里远吗?
Lí zhèlǐ yuǎn ma?

靠近火车站。
Kàojìn huǒchē zhàn.
It's near the train station.

Say: *Thank you.*

谢谢你。
Xièxie nǐ.

5 *square*

6 *museum*

1 Warm up

How do you say "bridge" and "fountain"? (pp.48–49)

Ask "Is it far from here?" (pp.48–49)

Ask "Is there a museum in town?" (pp.48–49)

问路 (wèn lù)
Asking for directions

Finding your way around a town in China can be confusing, so it is a good idea to learn how to ask for and understand directions. Chinese street names are written in characters along with pinyin transcription, so it's useful to familiarize yourself with both for your convenience.

2 Useful phrases

Practise these phrases and then test yourself.

左/右转 zuǒ/yòu zhuǎn	*turn left/right*
在左边。 Zài zuǒbiān.	*On the left.*
在右边。 Zài yòubiān.	*On the right.*
照直走。 Zhàozhí zǒu.	*Go straight on.*
请问，去宝塔怎么走? Qǐngwèn, qù bǎotǎ zěnme zǒu?	*Excuse me, how do I get to the pagoda?*
第一个街口，在左边。 Dì-yī gè jiēkǒu, zài zuǒbiān.	*First street on the left.*
第二个街口，在右边。 Dì-èr gè jiēkǒu, zài yòubiān.	*Second street on the right.*

公园 gōngyuán *park*

办公楼 bàngōnglóu *office bloc*

走到街角，左转。
Zǒudào jiējiǎo, zuǒ zhuǎn.
At the corner, turn left.

3 In conversation

请问，城里有餐馆吗?
Qǐngwèn, chéng lǐ yǒu cānguǎn ma?

Excuse me, is there a restaurant in town?

有，靠近火车站。
Yǒu, kàojìn huǒchē zhàn.

Yes there is, near the train station.

去火车站怎么走?
Qù huǒchē zhàn zěnme zǒu?

How do I get to the train station?

4 Words to remember

Familiarize yourself with these words and test yourself using the flap.

我迷路了。
Wǒ mílù le.
I'm lost.

traffic lights	红绿灯	hónglǜdēng
street corner	街角	jiējiǎo
street	街	jiē
road	路	lù
map	地图	dìtú
flyover	立交桥	lìjiāoqiáo
opposite	对面	duìmiàn
at the end of the street	这条街走到底	zhè tiáo jiē zǒu dàodǐ

5 Say it

At the traffic lights,
turn right.

At the station,
turn left.

It's about ten
minutes.

我们在哪里?
Wǒmen zài nǎli?
Where are we?

到了红绿灯，左转。
Dàole hónglǜdēng, zuǒ zhuǎn.

At the traffic lights, turn left.

远吗?
Yuǎn ma?

Is it far?

不远。大概五分钟。
Bùyuǎn. Dàgài wǔ fēnzhōng.

No, it's about five minutes.

1 Warm up

Say the days of the
week in Chinese.
(pp.28–29)

How do you say
"six o'clock"?
(pp.30–31)

Ask "What time is it?"
(pp.30–31)

观光 (guānguāng)
Sightseeing

Chinese shops are open late every day, closing
around 10 or 11pm and they operate seven
days a week. Tourist sights such as museums
are usually open all day from about 8am, but
may be closed during the lunch hour and for
one day a week, although this is not always
the case.

2 Words to remember

Familiarize yourself with these words and test yourself using the flap.

导游册 dǎoyóu cè	*guidebook*
免费（入场） miǎnfèi (rùchǎng)	*free (entrance)*
门票 ménpiào	*admission ticket*
禁止拍照 jìnzhǐ pāizhào	*cameras not allowed*
休息 xiūxi	*closed*

团体参观
tuántǐ cānguān
guided tour

Cultural tip China is a vast country, with its major cities growing so fast that
sightseeing often requires a lot of advance planning. Internal flights can be arranged
to take you between the different regions, but you will need permits to visit some
areas and it is best to check this out locally before you set off.

---

3 In conversation

你们今天下午开门
吗？
Nǐmen jīntiān xiàwǔ
kāimén ma?

*Do you open this
afternoon?*

是的，但我们六点钟
关门。
Shì de, dàn wǒmen liù
diǎnzhōng guānmén.

*Yes, but we close at
six o'clock.*

轮椅可以方便进出
吗？
Lúnyǐ kěyǐ fāngbiàn
jìnchū ma?

*Is wheelchair access
possible?*

4 Useful phrases

Learn these phrases and then test yourself using the cover flap.

	What time do you open?	你们什么时间开门？ Nǐmen shénme shíjiān kāimén?

| | *What time do you close?* | 你们什么时间关门？
Nǐmen shénme shíjiān guānmén? |

| | *Is wheelchair access possible?* | 轮椅可以方便进出吗？
Lúnyǐ kěyǐ fāngbiàn jìnchū ma? |

5 Put into practice

Cover the text on the right and complete the dialogue in Chinese.

对不起，博物馆关门了。
Duìbuqǐ, bówùguǎn guānmén le.
Sorry, the museum is closed.

Ask: Do you open on Sundays?

你们星期天开门吗？
Nǐmen xīngqītiān kāimén ma?

是的，但是关门时间比较早。
Shì de, dànshì guānmén shíjiān bǐjiào zǎo.
Yes, but we close early.

Ask: What time do you close?

你们什么时间关门？
Nǐmen shénme shíjiān guānmén?

可以，那边有电梯。
Kěyǐ, nàbiān yǒu diàntī.

Yes, there's a lift over there.

谢谢，我要买四张门票。
Xièxie, wǒ yào mǎi sì zhāng ménpiào.

Thank you. I'd like to buy four tickets.

这是您的门票，导游册免费。
Zhè shì nín de ménpiào, dǎoyóu cè miǎnfèi.

Here are your tickets. The guidebook is free.

1 Warm up

Say "Would you please help me?" (pp.24–25)

What's the Chinese for "ticket"? (pp.38–39)

Say "I'm going to Shanghai." (pp.40–41)

在机场 (zài jīchǎng)
At the airport

International flights arrive at most major cities, and there is an extensive network of internal flights operating from every provincial capital. Although the airport environment is largely universal, it is sometimes useful to be able to understand key words and phrases in Chinese.

2 Words to remember

Familiarize yourself with these words and test yourself using the flap.

办理登机手续 bànlǐ dēngjī shǒuxù	*check-in*
出发 chūfā	*departures*
到达 dàodá	*arrivals*
海关 hǎiguān	*customs*
边防检查 biānfáng jiǎnchá	*passport control*
候机楼 hòujīlóu	*terminal*
登机口 dēngjīkǒu	*gate*
航班 hángbān	*flight*
飞机 fēijī	*plane*

哪个登机口去香港?
Nǎge dēngjīkǒu qù
Xiānggǎng?
*Which gate is it for
Hong Kong?*

3 Useful phrases

Learn these phrases and then test yourself using the cover flap.

去伦敦的飞机准点 吗? Qù Lúndūn de fēijī zhǔndiǎn ma?	*Is the plane to London on time?*
我找不到我的行李。 Wǒ zhǎo bùdào wǒ de xíngli.	*I can't find my baggage.*
去上海的飞机晚点 了。 Qù Shànghǎi de fēijī wǎndiǎn le.	*The plane to Shanghai is delayed.*

4 Put into practice

Join in this conversation. Read the Chinese on the left and follow the instructions to make your reply. Then test yourself by concealing the answers with the cover flap.

下一位。
Xiàyīwèi.
Next, please.

Ask: Is the plane to Shanghai on time?

去上海的飞机准点吗?
Qù Shànghǎi de fēijī zhǔndiǎn ma?

的，准点。
Shì de, zhǔndiǎn.
Yes, it's on time.

Ask: Which gate is it?

哪个登机口?
Nǎge dēngjīkǒu?

5 Match and repeat

Match the numbered items to the Chinese words in the panel.

boarding pass ❶

ticket ❷

passport ❸

❹ *suitcase*

❺ *trolley*

1 登机牌
dēngjīpái

2 机票
jīpiào

3 护照
hùzhào

4 箱子
xiāngzi

5 手推车
shǒutuīchē

Read it

Chinese takes basic concepts and combines them to make different meanings, e.g. 飞机 feiji "plane" ("flying" fei + "machine" 机 ji); 火车 huoche "train" ("fire" 火 huo + "vehicle" 车 che).

答案(dá'àn)
Answers
Cover with flap

复习与重温(fùxí yǔ chóngwēn)
Review and repeat

1 Places

1 博物馆
bówùguǎn

2 斑马线
bānmǎxiàn

3 大桥
dàqiáo

4 宝塔
bǎotǎ

5 停车场
tíngchēchǎng

6 电影院
diànyǐngyuàn

7 广场
guǎngchǎng

1 Places

Name the numbered places in Chinese.

 ❶ museum

 ❷ crossing

 ❸ bridge

 ❹ pagoda

❺ car park

❻ cinema

❼ square

2 Car parts

1 挡风玻璃
dǎngfēng bōli

2 前灯
qiándēng

3 保险杠
bǎoxiǎngàng

4 车门
chēmén

5 车胎
chētāi

2 Car parts

Name these car parts in Chinese.

windscreen ❶

❺ tyre

door ❹

答案(dá'àn)
Answers
Cover with flap

3 Translation

What do these Chinese phrases mean?

1 zuo zhuan

2 Go and take cheng li you bowuguan ma

3 meiyou wangba

4 women zai nali

5 daqiao fujin you youyongchi

6 nimen shenme shijian kaimen

7 wo yao mai si zhang menpiao

3 Translation

1 *Turn left.*

2 *Is there a museum in town?*

3 *There isn't an internet café.*

4 *Where are we?*

5 *There's a swimming pool near the bridge.*

6 *What time do you open?*

7 *I'd like four tickets.*

2 *headlight*

3 *bumper*

4 Directions

Ask how to get to these places:

1 *pagoda*

2 *train station*

3 *internet café*

4 *cinema*

4 Directions

1 去宝塔怎么走?
Qù bǎotǎ zěnme zǒu?

2 去火车站怎么走?
Qù huǒchē zhàn zěnme zǒu?

3 去网吧怎么走?
Qù wǎngbā zěnme zǒu?

4 去电影院怎么走?
Qù diànyǐngyuàn zěnme zǒu?

1 Warm up

Ask "How much is that?" (pp.18–19)

What are "breakfast", "lunch", and "dinner"? (pp.20–21)

What are "three", "four", "five", and "six"? (pp.10–11)

订房间 (dìng fángjiān)
Booking a room

Large and medium-sized cities have a considerable number of international hotels as well as traditional Chinese spas. Most hotels are star-rated, and Western tourists will generally find that hotels with a minimum of a three-star rating will meet their expected standards.

2 Useful phrases

Practise these phrases and then test yourself by concealing the Chinese on the left with the cover flap.

房价包含早餐吗?
Fángjià bāohán zǎocān ma?

Is breakfast included? (Does the room include breakfast?)

房间里能上网吗?
Fángjiàn lǐ néng shàngwǎng ma?

Does the room have internet access?

有送餐服务吗?
Yǒu sòngcān fúwù ma?

Is there room service?

最迟几点钟退房?
Zuìchí jǐ diǎnzhōng tuìfáng?

What time is checkout?

3 In conversation

有空房间吗?
Yǒu kòng fángjiān ma?

Do you have any rooms?

有。我们有一间双人房。
Yǒu. Wǒmen yǒu yī jiān shuāngrén fáng.

Yes, we have a double room.

有送餐服务吗?
Yǒu sòngcān fúwù ma?

Is there room service?

4 Words to remember

Familiarize yourself with these words and test yourself by concealing the Chinese on the right with the cover flap.

room	房间	fángjiān
single room	单人房	dānrén fáng
double room	双人房	shuāngrén fáng
lift	电梯	diàntī
bathroom	卫生间	wèishēngjiān
shower	淋浴	línyù
breakfast	早餐	zǎocān
key	钥匙	yàoshi
balcony	阳台	yángtái
two nights	两天	liǎng tiān
three nights	三天	sān tiān

房间里能看到海景吗?
Fángjiān lǐ néng kàndào hǎijǐng ma?
Does the room have a sea view?

5 Say it

Do you have any single rooms?

Two nights.

Is dinner included?

Cultural tip Chinese hotel rooms tend to include a pair of house slippers as a matter of course. You are assumed to want to remove your shoes in the room as you would at home. Toothbrushes and toothpaste are also provided.

有。您要住几天?
Yǒu. Nín yào zhù jǐ tiān?

Yes, there is. How many nights?

三天。
Sān tiān.

Three nights.

好了。这是您的钥匙。
Hǎo le. Zhè shì nín de yàoshi.

Very good. Here's your key.

1 Warm up

How do you say "Is/Are there...?", "There is/are...", and "There isn't/aren't..."? (pp.48–49)

What's the Chinese for "room"? (pp.58–59)

在酒店 (zài jiǔdiàn)
In the hotel

Most of the new hotels designed for foreign tourists and business people are modelled on standard international hotel chains. Those rated three-star or above usually provide a broadband internet connection in the room, free of charge.

2 Match and repeat

Match the numbered items in this hotel bedroom with the Chinese text in the panel and test yourself using the cover flap.

1 床头柜
chuángtóuguì

2 电灯
diàndēng

3 窗帘
chuānglián

4 沙发
shāfā

5 枕头
zhěntou

6 床
chuáng

7 床单
chuángdān

8 毛毯
máotǎn

1 *bedside table*

2 *lamp*

3 *curtains*

sofa 4

6 *bed*

blanket 8

5 *pillow*

7 *bedspread*

Cultural tip It's common to find a flask of hot water in your room to make tea or simply drink by itself. Room service should be able to refill the flask if it runs out. Bottled water is also sometimes provided free of charge. In common with most international hotels, hotels in China add a surcharge for using the telephone.

3 Useful phrases

Learn these phrases and then test yourself using the cover flap.

The room is too hot.

房间里太热。
Fángjiān lǐ tài rè.

The room is too cold.

房间里太冷。
Fángjiān lǐ tài lěng.

There aren't any towels.

没有毛巾了。
Méiyǒu máojīn le.

I'd like some soap.

我要一块肥皂。
Wǒ yào yī kuài féizào.

The shower is broken.

淋浴坏了。
Línyù huài le.

4 Put into practice

Cover the text on the right and then complete the dialogue in Chinese.

你好，我是前台。
Nǐ hǎo, wǒ shì qiántái.
Hello, this is the front desk.

Say: There aren't any pillows.

没有枕头了。
Méiyǒu zhěntou le.

工作人员很快就
会给您送去。
Gōngzuò rényuán
hěn kuài jiùhuì gěi
nín sòngqù.
The staff will bring you some.

Say: And also, the room is too hot.

还有，房间里太热。
Háiyǒu, fángjiān lǐ tài rè.

1 Warm up

What is Chinese for "shower" (pp.60–61), and "swimming pool"? (pp.48–49)

Say "I'd like some towels." (pp.60–61)

温泉度假 (wēnquán dùjià)
Hot spas

Many tourist spots in China feature **wenquan dujia** (*hot spas*), combined with accommodation at times. You can experience traditional Chinese beauty and healing treatments, which emphasize the balance between **yin** and **yang** and advocate natural ways to boost **qi** (vitality inside the body).

2 Match and repeat

Learn these words and then test yourself by concealing the Chinese with the cover flap.

1 阳伞
  yángsǎn

2 晨衣
  chényī

3 蜡烛
  làzhú

4 床旗
  chuángqí

5 拖鞋
  tuōxié

6 足疗
  zúliáo

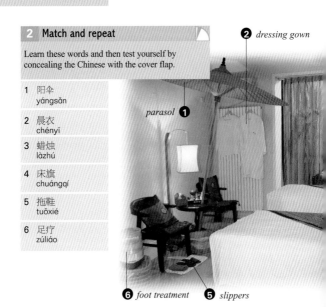

❷ *dressing gown*

parasol **❶**

❻ *foot treatment*   **❺** *slippers*

3 In conversation

有哪些疗法呢?
Yǒu nǎxiē liáofǎ ne?

What kind of treatments are there?

可以做按摩, 也可以洗温泉浴。
Kěyǐ zuò ànmó, yě kěyǐ xǐ wēnquányù.

You can have a massage or a hot spa bath.

一次需要多长时间
Yī cì xūyào duōcháng shíjiān.

How long will the treatment take?

4 Useful phrases

Learn these phrases. Read the English under the pictures and say the phrase in Chinese as shown on the right. Then cover up the answers on the right and test yourself.

5 Say it

Can I have a hot spa bath?

What kind of massages are there?

I'd like a foot massage.

3 candle

bed runner 4

How long will the treatment take?

一次需要多长时间?
Yī cì xūyào duōcháng shíjiān?

Can I have acupuncture?

可以针灸吗?
Kěyǐ zhēnjiǔ ma?

Can I have a herbal foot massage?

可以药物洗脚吗?
Kěyǐ yàowù xǐjiǎo ma?

These herbs are fragrant.

这草药味道很香。
Zhè cǎoyào wèidào hěn xiāng.

有一小时的, 也有两小时的。
Yǒu yī xiǎoshí de, yě yǒu liǎng xiǎoshí de.

There are one-hour or two-hour (sessions).

很贵吗?
Hěn guì ma?

Is it very expensive?

不贵, 一小时350元。
Bù guì, yī xiǎoshí sānbǎi wǔshí yuán.

It's not expensive, 350 yuan per hour.

1 Warm up

How do you say "My son has a car"? (pp.14–15)

What is the Chinese for "room", "bed", and "pillow"? (pp.60–61)

形容词 (xíngróngcí)
Adjectives

Basic adjectives (descriptive words) are quite straightforward in Chinese: *car(s)* is **qiche**; *small car(s)* is **xiao qiche**. A simple way to describe things is to use the word **hen**, which carries the meaning of *very*: **zhe qiche hen xiao** *"This car is (very) small"*, **shan hen gao** *"The mountains are (very) high"*.

2 Words to remember

There are no plurals in Chinese. So "the mountain is (very) high" and "the mountains are (very) high" would both be **shan hen gao**.

大 dà	*big, large*
小 xiǎo	*small*
高 gāo	*high, tall*
低 dī	*low*
热 rè	*hot*
冷 lěng	*cold*
安静 ānjìng	*quiet*
吵闹 chǎonào	*noisy*
硬 yìng	*hard*
软 ruǎn	*soft*
美 měi	*beautiful*

宝塔很古老。
Bǎotǎ hěn gǔlǎo.
The pagoda is (very) old.

树很美。
Shù hěn měi.
The trees are (very) beautiful.

Read it The first two adjectives above — 大 da, "big", and 小 xiao, "small" — are amongst the easiest Chinese characters to recognize. They originate from representations of a person holding arms out wide ("big") and pointing down by the side ("small"). These characters combine with others, for example 小鼠 xiao-shu means "mouse" ("small rat"); 大衣 da-yi means "coat" ("big jacket").

3 Useful phrases

Learn these useful descriptive phrases and then test yourself using the cover flap.

The coffee is cold.

咖啡冷了。
Kāfēi lěng le.

My room is very noisy.

我的房间很吵闹。
Wǒ de fángjiān hěn chǎonào.

This car is very small.

这汽车很小。
Zhè qìchē hěn xiǎo.

This bed is very hard.

这床很硬。
Zhè chuáng hěn yìng.

4 Put into practice

Join in this conversation. Cover up the text on the right and complete the dialogue in Chinese. Check and repeat if necessary.

房间在这里。
Fángjiān zài zhèlǐ.
Here's the room.

景色很美。
Jǐngsè hěn měi.

Say: The view is very beautiful.

卫生间在那里。
Wèishēngjiān zài nàlǐ.
The bathroom is over there.

房间很小。
Fángjiān hěn xiǎo.

Say: The room is very small.

可惜，没有其他房间了。
Kěxī, méiyǒu qítā fángjiān le.
Unfortunately, there aren't any other rooms.

我们就要它。
Wǒmen jiùyào tā.

Say: We'll take it.

复习与重温(fùxí yǔ chóngwēn)
Review and repeat

答案(dá'àn)
Answers
Cover with flap

1 Adjectives

1 大
  dà

2 软
  ruǎn

3 古老
  gǔlǎo

4 安静
  ānjìng

5 冷
  lěng

1 Adjectives

Put the word in brackets into Chinese.

1 zhe qiche hen _____ (big)

2 zhe chuang hen _____ (soft)

3 baota hen _____ (old) ma

4 wo de fangjian hen _____ (quiet)

5 cha _____ (cold) le

2 Spas

1 足疗
  zúliáo

2 拖鞋
  tuōxié

3 阳伞
  yángsǎn

4 晨衣
  chényī

5 蜡烛
  làzhú

6 床旗
  chuángqí

2 Spas

Name these items you might find in a traditional Chinese spa.

1 *foot treatment*

2 *slippers*

3 *parasol*

4 *dressing gown*

答案(dá'àn)
Answers
Cover with flap

3 At the hotel

You are booking a room in a hotel. Follow the conversation, replying in Chinese using the English prompts.

nihao
1 *Do you have any rooms?*

nin yao zhu ji tian
2 *Five nights.*

hao le
3 *Is breakfast included?*

fangjian baohan zaocan
4 *We'll take it.*

3 At the hotel

1 有空房间吗?
Yǒu kòng fángjiān
ma?

2 五天。
Wǔ tiān.

3 房价包含早餐吗?
Fángjià bāohán
zǎocān ma?

4 我们就要它。
Wǒmen jiùyào tā.

5 candle

bed runner 6

4 Negatives

Make these sentences negative using **bu** or **mei.**

1 wo shi Zhongguoren

2 wo you san ge haizi

3 fujin you wangba

4 Han Hong shi xuesheng

5 women you kafei

4 Negatives

1 我不是中国人。
Wǒ bù shì
Zhōngguórén.

2 我没有三个孩
子。
Wǒ méiyǒu sān gè
háizi.

3 附近没有网吧
吗?
Fùjìn méiyǒu
wǎngbā ma?

4 韩红不是学生。
Hán Hóng bù
shì xuéshēng.

5 我们没有咖啡。
Wǒmen méiyǒu
kāfēi.

1 Warm up

Ask "Can I use a credit card?" (p.39)

Say "At the traffic lights, turn left", and "The station is near the café." (pp.50–51)

百货商店 (bǎihuò shāngdiàn)
Department store

Department stores are sometimes referred to as **baihuo dalou** (*"big building department stores"*) since they tend to be landmark buildings in city centres, selling everything from clothes to musical instruments. The concept is changing as shopping malls have mushroomed in many Chinese cities.

2 Match and repeat

Notice the Chinese word 类 lei, meaning *category*: jiu lei, *spirit category (off-licence)*; yu lei, *fish category (fishmonger)*, etc. Match the shops below to the Chinese words in the panel on the left.

1 面包类
  miànbāo lèi

2 糕点类
  gāodiǎn lèi

3 酒类
  jiǔ lèi

4 熟食类
  shúshí lèi

5 蔬菜类
  shūcài lèi

6 图书类
  túshū lèi

7 鱼类
  yú lèi

8 肉类
  ròu lèi

9 豆制品类
  dòuzhìpǐn lèi

❶ baker

❷ cake shop

❹ delicatessen

❺ greengrocer

❼ fishmonger

❽ butcher

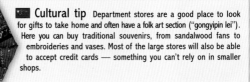

Cultural tip Department stores are a good place to look for gifts to take home and often have a folk art section ("gongyipin lei"). Here you can buy traditional souvenirs, from sandalwood fans to embroideries and vases. Most of the large stores will also be able to accept credit cards — something you can't rely on in smaller shops.

3 Words to remember

Familiarize yourself with these words and then test yourself.

dairy	乳制品 rǔzhìpǐn
antique shop	古董店 gǔdǒngdiàn
hairdresser	美发店 měifàdiàn
barber	理发店 lǐfàdiàn
jeweller	珠宝店 zhūbǎodiàn
post office	邮局 yóujú
florist	花卉店 huāhuìdiàn
shoe shop	鞋店 xiédiàn
travel agent	旅行社 lǚxíngshè

哪里有花卉店?
Nǎli yǒu huāhuìdiàn?
Can you tell me where the florist is?

3 *off-licence*

6 *bookshop*

9 *tofu shop*

4 Useful phrases

Familiarize yourself with these phrases.

Can you tell me where the hairdresser is?	哪里有美发店? Nǎli yǒu měifàdiàn?
Where can I pay?	在哪里付钱? Zài nǎli fùqián?
I'm just looking, thanks.	我只想看看, 谢谢。 Wǒ zhǐxiǎng kànkan, xièxie.
Where can I buy phonecards?	哪里可以买到电话卡? Nǎli kěyǐ mǎidào diànhuàkǎ?
Can I exchange this?	我可以更换它吗? Wǒ kěyǐ gēnghuàn tā ma?
I'd like a receipt, please?	请给我一张发票, 好吗? Qǐng gěi wǒ yī zhāng fāpiào, hǎo ma?
I'd like to place an order for...	我想订购一个…… Wǒ xiǎng dìnggòu yī gè...

5 Say it

Can you tell me where the baker is?

Where can I buy fish?

I'd like to place an order for curtains.

1 Warm up

What are "forty", "seventy", "a hundred", "a thousand", and "ten thousand" in Chinese? (pp.30–31)

Say "big" and "small" in Chinese. (pp.64–65)

电器商店 (diànqì shāngdiàn)
Electronics store

The Chinese are catching up with the West, in terms of electrical and electronic consumer goods. In every mall and large department store, there's bound to be a store or department selling computers, mobile phones, digital cameras, etc. Power rates in China are 220V/50Hz.

2 Match and repeat

Match the numbered items to the Chinese words in the panel on the left and test yourself using the cover flap.

1 鼠标
shǔbiāo

2 适配器
shìpèiqì

3 变压器
biànyāqì

4 笔记本电脑
bǐjìběn diànnǎo

5 屏幕
píngmù

6 保修证
bǎoxiūzhèng

7 内存
nèicún

8 电池
diànchí

> **Read it** When you see price labels, you will usually see the symbol for "yuan" ¥ followed by the price in Western figures or sometimes the price followed by the Chinese character 元.

> ¥5800   50元

❶ mouse
transformer ❸
adapter ❷
memory ❼
❽ battery
guarantee ❻

3 In conversation

这台笔记本电脑多少钱?
Zhè tái bǐjìběn diànnǎo duōshao qián?

How much is that laptop computer?

5800 元。
Wǔqiān bābǎi yuán.

It's 5,800 yuan.

硬盘空间有多大?
Yìngpán kōngjiān yǒu duōdà?

How big is the hard drive?

Cultural tip The Chinese currency is called "Renminbi" (literally "people's money") and the unit is the yuan. The highest denomination banknote is 100 yuan. Although this may not seem like a large amount when you exchange currency, 100 yuan can still go a long way in China.

④ laptop

⑤ screen

Useful phrases

Learn these phrases. Then conceal the answers on the right using the cover flap. Read the English under the pictures and say the phrase in Chinese as shown on the right.

That camera is too expensive.

这架相机太贵。
Zhè jià xiàngjī tài guì.

How much is that one?

这款多少钱?
Zhè kuǎn duōshao qián?

Will it work in England?

在英国能用吗?
Zài Yīngguó néng yòng ma?

40吉兆,一吉兆内存。
Sìshí jízhào, yī jízhào nèicún.

40 gigabytes, and one gigabyte of memory.

在英国能用吗?
Zài Yīngguó néng yòngma?

Will it work in England?

能用。但是需要一个变压器。
Néng yòng. Dànshì xūyào yī gè biànyāqì.

Yes it will, but you need a transformer.

1 Warm up

What are these items which you could buy in a supermarket? (pp.22–23)

shuiguo
mifan
shucai
miantiao
yu
rou

在超市 (zài chāoshì)
At the supermarket

In recent years, many multinational super market operators have entered the Chinese market. Familiar names can be found in every large and medium-sized city in China. The layout is similar to Western supermarkets but with a blend of Chinese and imported goods available.

2 Match and repeat

Look at the numbered items and match them to the Chinese words in the panel on the left.

1 饮料
  yǐnliào

2 化妆品
  huàzhuāngpǐn

3 小吃
  xiǎochī

4 冷冻食品
  lěngdòng shípǐn

5 蔬菜
  shūcài

6 即食食品
  jíshí shípǐn

7 家庭用品
  jiātíng yòngpǐn

8 水果
  shuǐguǒ

drinks ❶

fruit ❽

household products ❼

ready meals ❻

vegetables ❺

❹ *frozen foods*

Cultural tip Supermarkets usually pre-package fresh produce such as meat, fish, fruit, vegetables, and soybean products. You just pick up the pre-priced packet you want and take it to the checkout counter.

3 Useful phrases

Learn these phrases and then test yourself using the cover flap.

I'd like a bag, please.

请给我一个塑料袋，好吗？
Qǐng gěi wǒ yī gè sùliàodài, hǎo ma?

Where is the drinks section?

饮料在什么地方？
Yǐnliào zài shénme dìfāng?

Where's the checkout counter?

在哪儿付款？
Zài nǎr fùkuǎn?

Where are the shopping trolleys?

哪儿有手推车？
Nǎr yǒu shǒutuīchē?

4 Words to remember

Learn these words and then test yourself using the cover flap.

2 *beauty products*

3 *snacks*

bread	面包	miànbāo
milk	牛奶	niúnǎi
butter	黄油	huángyóu
dairy products	乳制品	rǔzhìpǐn
ham	火腿	huǒtuǐ
salt	盐	yán
pepper	胡椒	hújiāo
toilet paper	卫生纸	wèishēngzhǐ
nappies	尿片	niàopiàn
washing-up liquid	洗洁精	xǐjiéjīng

5 Say it

Where is the snacks section?

I'd like some butter, please?

Is there any ham?

衣服和鞋子 (yīfu hé xiézi)
Clothes and shoes

A vast variety of clothing to suit all styles and budgets is now available in China, both in the clothing sections of shopping centres and department stores and in local markets. Except in some of the more rural areas, the traditional dress is now mainly seen only in films and at the Chinese opera.

2 Match and repeat

Match the numbered items of clothing to the Chinese words in the panel on the left. Test yourself using the cover flap.

1 衬衫
  chènshān

2 领带
  lǐngdài

3 袖子
  xiùzi

4 夹克衫
  jiākèshān

5 衣袋
  yīdài

6 裤子
  kùzi

7 裙子
  qúnzi

8 裤袜
  kùwà

9 鞋子
  xiézi

shirt ❶

tie ❷

sleeve ❸

jacket ❹

pocket ❺

trousers ❻

Cultural tip China has different systems of sizes. Often clothes sizes are given in a combination of height (in metres) and chest size, or by using the general size indicators (XL,L,M,S,XS, etc.). Even allowing for conversion of sizes, Chinese clothes, and especially shoes, tend to be smaller than their Western equivalents.

3 Useful phrases

Learn these phrases and then test yourself using the cover flap.

Do you have a larger size?

有大一号的吗？
Yǒu dà yīhào de ma?

It's not what I want.

这不是我想要的。
Zhè bù shì wǒ xiǎng yào de .

I'll take the pink one.

我要粉红色的。
Wǒ yào fěnhóng sè de.

4 Words to remember

Colours are adjectives (see p.64). Below, you will see the pure form of the colours, but often the character 色 **se** and/or 的 **de** is added depending on the sentence.

red/pink	红/ 粉红 hóng/ fěnhóng
white	白 bái
blue	蓝 lán
yellow	黄 huáng
green	绿 lǜ
black	黑 hēi

7 *skirt*

8 *tights*

9 *shoes*

Read it The characters for colours are worth recognizing and they can often be seen in combination: 白酒 "baijui" white liquor; 红茶 "hongcha" red tea; 黄油 "huangyou" butter ("yellow fat"); 蓝图 "lantu" blueprint ("blue picture").

答案(dá'àn)
Answers
Cover with flap

复习与重温(fùxí yǔ chóngwēn)
Review and repeat

1 Electronic

1 鼠标
shǔbiāo

2 适配器
shìpèiqì

3 变压器
biànyāqì

4 屏幕
píngmù

5 电池
diànchí

6 内存
nèicún

7 保修证
bǎoxiūzhèng

8 笔记本电脑
bǐjìběn diànnǎo

1 Electronic

Name the numbered items in Chinese.

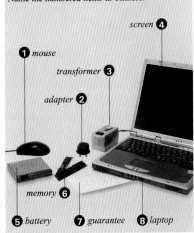

- screen **4**
- **1** mouse
- transformer **3**
- adapter **2**
- memory **6**
- **5** battery
- **7** guarantee
- **8** laptop

2 Description

1 *That camera is too expensive.*

2 *My room is very noisy.*

3 *Do you have a larger size?*

2 Description

What do these phrases mean?

1 zhe jia xiangji tai gui

2 wo de fangjian hen chaonao

3 you da yihao de ma

3 Shops

1 面包类
miànbāo lèi

2 熟食类
shúshí lèi

3 蔬菜类
shūcài lèi

4 鱼类
yú lèi

5 糕点类
gāodiǎn lèi

6 肉类
ròu lèi

3 Shops

Name the numbered shops in Chinese. Then check your answers.

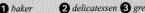

1 baker **2** delicatessen **3** greengrocer

4 fishmonger **5** cake shop **6** butcher

答案(dá'àn)
Answers
Cover with flap

Supermarket

What is the Chinese for the numbered product categories?

1 *drinks*

2 *household products*

3 *beauty products*

4 *frozen foods*

5 *snacks*

Supermarket

1 饮料
yǐnliào

2 家庭用品
jiātíng yòngpǐn

3 化妆品
huàzhuāngpǐn

4 冷冻食品
lěngdòng shípǐn

5 小吃
xiǎochī

Museum

Join in this conversation replying in Chinese following the English prompts.

nihao
1 *I'd like to buy four tickets.*

zhe shi nin de menpiao
2 *What time do you close?*

women liu dianzhong guanmen
3 *Is there a guidebook?*

you. daoyou ce mianfei
4 *Where's the lift?*

nabian you dianti
5 *Thank you.*

Museum

1 我要买四张门票。
Wǒ yào mǎi sì zhāng ménpiào.

2 你们什么时间关门?
Nǐmen shénme shíjiān guānmén?

3 有导游册吗?
Yǒu dǎoyóu cè ma?

4 电梯在哪里?
Diàntī zài nǎli?

5 谢谢你。
Xièxie nǐ.

Say "Han Hong is a student" and "I'm English." (pp.14–15)

Say "The internet café is in the centre of town." (pp.48–49)

工作 (gōngzuò)
Jobs

Many Chinese words that are used to refer to occupations have the character 师 **shi** *("master")* or 生 **sheng** *("person")* at the end. The leader or head of a unit is indicated by the character 长 **zhang**. Businesses often have a tight hierarchy (see Cultural tip on p.79).

2 Words to remember: jobs

Familiarize yourself with these Chinese words and test yourself using the flap.

医生 yīshēng	*doctor*
牙医 yáyī	*dentist*
护士 hùshi	*nurse*
老师 lǎoshī	*teacher*
会计师 kuàijìshī	*accountant*
律师 lǜshī	*lawyer*
设计师 shèjìshī	*designer*
秘书 mìshū	*secretary*
店主 diànzhǔ	*shopkeeper*
工程师 gōngchéngshī	*engineer*
管道工 guǎndàogōng	*plumber*
厨师 chúshī	*cook*
个体户 gètǐhù	*self-employed*
学生 xuéshēng	*student*

我是商人。
Wǒ shì shāngrén.
I'm a business person.

我是会计师。
Wǒ shì kuàijìshī.
I'm an accountant.

3 Put into practice

Join in this conversation. Use the cover flap to conceal the text on the right and complete the dialogue in Chinese.

您做什么工作?
Nín zuò shénme gōngzuò?
What's your profession?

Say: I'm a designer.

我是设计师。
Wǒ shì shèjìshī.

您在哪个公司工作?
Nín zài nǎge gōngsī gōngzuò?
What company do you work for?

Say: I'm self-employed.

我是个体户。
Wǒ shì gètǐhù.

哦, 是这样。
Ò, shì zhèyàng.
Oh, I see.

Ask: What's your profession?

您做什么工作?
Nín zuò shénme gōngzuò?

Cultural tip There are different titles for "manager" depending on the level. The order of seniority is 总经理 zongjingli (MD), 部门总监 bumen zongjian (director), 处长 chuzhang (head of division), 科长 kezhang (head of unit), 组长 zuzhang (group leader). Look out for the titles on business cards.

4 Words to remember: workplace

Familiarize yourself with these words and test yourself.

总部在上海。
Zǒngbù zài Shànghǎi.
The head office is in Shanghai.

head office	总部	zǒngbù
branch	分支机构	fēnzhī jīgòu
department	部	bù
office worker	办公人员	bàngōng rényuán
manager	经理	jīnglǐ

1 Warm up

Practise different ways of introducing yourself in different situations (pp.8–9). Mention your name, occupation, and any other information you'd like to volunteer (pp.12–13, pp.14–15).

办公室 (bàngōngshì)
The office

Traditionally, most adult Chinese would have a **sizhang**, an official seal or stamp bearing their name in characters. You may still see these stamps on official government papers and high-level contracts, although they are no longer the necessity they once were.

2 Words to remember

Familiarize yourself with these words. Read them aloud several times and try to memorize them. Conceal the Chinese with the cover flap and test yourself.

计算机 jìsuànjī	*computer*
鼠标 shǔbiāo	*mouse*
电子邮件 diànzǐ yóujiàn	*e-mail*
因特网 yīntèwǎng	*internet*
密码 mìmǎ	*password*
语音邮件 yǔyīn yóujiàn	*voicemail*
传真 chuánzhēn	*fax*
复印 fùyìn	*photocopy*
复印机 fùyìnjī	*photocopier*
书 shū	*book*
日志 rìzhì	*diary*
名片 míngpiàn	*business card*
会议 huìyì	*meeting*
研讨会 yántǎohuì	*conference*
会议日程 huìyì rìchéng	*agenda*

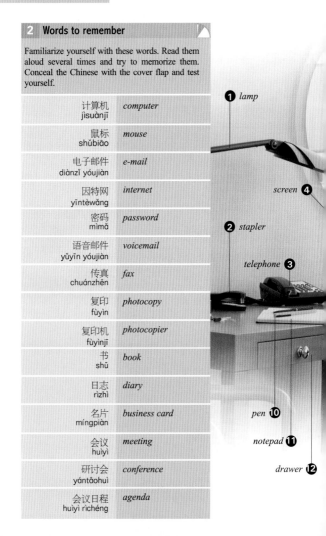

❶ lamp

screen ❹

❷ stapler

telephone ❸

pen ❿

notepad ⓫

drawer ⓬

3 Useful phrases

Learn these phrases and then test yourself using the cover flap.

I need to make some photocopies.

我需要复印资料。
Wǒ xūyào fùyìn zīliào.

I'd like to arrange an appointment.

我想安排一次见面。
Wǒ xiǎng ānpái yī cì jiànmiàn.

I want to send an e-mail.

我要发送电子邮件。
Wǒ yào fāsòng diànzǐ yóujiàn.

4 Match and repeat

Match the numbered items to the Chinese words on the right.

5 *keyboard*

6 *laptop*

printer **9**

7 *desk*

8 *clock*

13 *swivel chair*

1 灯
dēng

2 订书机
dìngshūjī

3 电话
diànhuà

4 屏幕
píngmù

5 键盘
jiànpán

6 笔记本电脑
bǐjìběn diànnǎo

7 办公桌
bàngōngzhuō

8 闹钟
nàozhōng

9 打印机
dǎyìnjī

10 笔
bǐ

11 书写纸
shūxiězhǐ

12 抽屉
chōutì

13 坐椅
zuòyǐ

5 Say it

I'd like to arrange a meeting.

I want to send a fax.

Is there an agenda?

1 Warm up

Say "Oh, I see!"
(pp.78–79), "meeting"
(pp.80–81), and
appointment".
(pp.32–33)

Ask "What's your
profession?" and
answer "I'm a lawyer."
(pp.78–79)

在研讨会上
(zài yántǎohuì shàng)
At the conference

University courses usually last four years and
entrance to the top colleges is very competitive.
High schools often start to prepare for the
entrance exam many years in advance as future
prospects can depend on which university a
student attends. Once there, the pressure is less
intense.

2 Useful phrases

Learn these phrases and then test yourself using the cover flap.

您是搞什么专业的? Nín shì gǎo shénme zhuānyè de?	*What's your field?*	
我是搞研究的。 Wǒ shì gǎo yánjiū de.	*I'm doing research.*	
我有法学学位。 Wǒ yǒu fǎxué xuéwèi.	*I have a degree in law.*	
我是建筑学讲师。 Wǒ shì jiànzhùxué jiǎngshī.	*I'm a lecturer in architecture.*	

3 In conversation

你好，我是严俊盟。
Nǐhǎo, wǒ shì Yán
Jùnméng.

*Hello, I'm Yan
Junmeng.*

您在哪个大学任教?
Nín zài nǎge dàxué
rènjiào?

*Which university do
you teach at?*

我在北京大学任教。
Wǒ zài Běijīng Dàxué
rènjiào.

*I teach at Beijing
University.*

4 Words to remember

Familiarize yourself with these words and then test yourself.

conference (academic)	研讨会 yántǎohuì
lecture	讲课 jiǎngkè
seminar	讲座 jiǎngzuò
lecture theatre	教室 jiàoshì
exhibition	展示会 zhǎnshìhuì
university lecturer	大学讲师 dàxué jiǎngshī
professor	教授 jiàoshòu
medicine	医科 yīkē
science	理科 lǐkē
literature	文科 wénkē
engineering	工科 gōngkē
law	法律 fǎlǜ
architecture	建筑学 jiànzhùxué
information technology	"IT" IT

我们的展台在那边。
Wǒmen de zhǎntái zài nàbiān.
There's our exhibition stand.

5 Say it

I teach at London University.

I have a degree in medicine.

I'm a lecturer in engineering.

您是搞什么专业的?
Nín shì gǎo shénme zhuānyè de?

What's your field?

物理学。我也做研究。
Wùlǐxué. Wǒ yě zuò yánjiū.

Physics. I'm also doing research.

哦,是这样。
Ò, shì zhèyàng.

Oh, I see.

洽谈业务 (qiàtán yèwù)
In business

You will make a good impression if you make the effort to begin a meeting with a few words in Chinese, even if your vocabulary is limited. After that, all parties will probably be happy to continue in English. Remember to take business cards to exchange at meetings.

2 Words to remember

Familiarize yourself with these words and then test yourself by concealing the Chinese with the cover flap.

订单 dìngdān	*order*
交付 jiāofù	*delivery*
付款 fùkuǎn	*payment*
预算 yùsuàn	*budget*
价格 jiàgé	*price*
文件 wénjiàn	*documents*
发票 fāpiào	*invoice*
估算 gūsuàn	*estimate*
利润 lìrùn	*profits*
销售 xiāoshòu	*sales*
总计 zǒngjì	*figures*

顾客
gùkè
client

报告书
bàogàoshū
report

Cultural tip In general, business dealings are formal. However, the Chinese are famous for their hospitality. There's always an exchange of gifts at the end of a business meeting, so don't forget to bring something from home to show your appreciation.

3 | Useful phrases

Practise these phrases. Note that the Chinese is necessarily very polite. It's better to err on the side of caution in a business context.

请给我看合同，好吗?
Qǐng gěi wǒ kàn hétong, hǎo ma?
Please show me the contract.

总经理
zǒngjīnglǐ
managing director

Can you send me the contract, please?

请把合同送给我，好吗?
Qǐng bǎ hétong sònggěi wǒ, hǎo ma?

我们商定价格了吗?
Wǒmen shāngdìng jiàgé le ma?

Have we agreed a price?

你们什么时候能交付?
Nǐmen shénme shíhou néng jiāofù?

When can you make the delivery?

预算是多少?
Yùsuàn shì duōshao?

How much is the budget?

4 | Say it

Can you send me the invoice, please?

What's the price?

Please show me the order.

⊞ Read it Some Chinese characters often re-occur in different combinations. Two of these are 机 ji, meaning "machine" or "device", and 电 dian, meaning "electric":

电话机 dianhuaji *telephone ("electric speaking machine")*

电脑 diannao *computer ("electric brain")*

电视机 dianshiji *television ("electric watching machine")*

复印机 fuyinji *photocopier ("copy machine")*

打印机 dayinji *printer ("printing machine")*

答案(dá'àn)
Answers
Cover with flap

复习与重温(fùxí yǔ chóngwēn)
Review and repeat

1 At the office

1 灯
dēng

2 笔记本电脑
bǐjìběn diànnǎo

3 笔
bǐ

4 订书机
dìngshūjī

5 办公桌
bàngōngzhuō

6 书写纸
shūxiězhǐ

7 闹钟
nàozhōng

1 At the office

Name these items in Chinese.

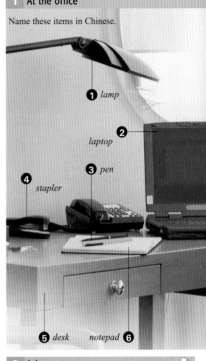

1 *lamp*

2 *laptop*

3 *pen*

4 *stapler*

5 *desk*　*notepad* **6**

2 Jobs

1 医生
yīshēng

2 管道工
guǎndàogōng

3 店主
diànzhǔ

4 会计师
kuàijìshī

5 学生
xuéshēng

6 律师
lǜshī

2 Jobs

What are these jobs in Chinese?

1 *doctor*

2 *plumber*

3 *shopkeeper*

4 *accountant*

5 *student*

6 *lawyer*

答案(dá'àn)
Answers
Cover with flap

clock **7**

3 Work

Answer these
questions following
the English prompts.

**nin zuo shenme
gongzuo**
1 *Say "I'm a
dentist."*

**nin zai nage gongsi
gongzuo**
2 *Say "I'm self-
employed."*

**nin zai nage daxue
renjiao**
3 *Say "I teach
at Beijing
University."*

wei, wo shi zongji
4 *Say "I'd like to
arrange an
appointment."*

3 Work

1 我是牙医。
Wǒ shì yáyī.

2 我是个体户。
Wǒ shì gètǐhù.

3 我在北京大学任
教。
Wǒ zài Běijīng
Dàxué rènjiào.

4 我想安排一次见面。
Wǒ xiǎng ānpái yī cì
jiànmiàn.

4 How much?

Answer the question with the price shown in
brackets.

1 **kafei duoshao qian**
(¥30)

2 **fangjian duoshao qian**
(¥800)

3 **diannao duoshao qian**
(¥10,000)

4 **chepiao duoshao qian**
(¥70)

4 How much?

1 三百元
sānbǎi yuán

2 八百元
bābǎi yuán

3 一万元
yīwàn yuán

4 七十元
qīshí yuán

1 Warm up

Say "Can you give me the receipt?" (pp.68–69)

Ask "Do you have any cakes?" (pp.18–19)

在药房 (zài yàofáng)
At the chemist

You may be asked **nali bu shufu** *(what's the matter?)*. To describe an ailment you can use the phrase **wo ... teng** *(I have a ... ache)*: **wo tou teng** *(I have a headache)*; **wo wei teng** *(I have a stomachache)*. Notice that the ailment or part of the body appears in the middle of the sentence.

2 Match and repeat

Match the numbered items to the Chinese words in the panel on the left and test yourself using the cover flap.

1 绷带
  bēngdài

2 糖浆
  tángjiāng

3 药水
  yàoshuǐ

4 创可贴
  chuāngkětiē

5 注射器
  zhùshèqì

6 药片
  yàopiàn

7 栓剂
  shuānjì

8 药膏
  yàogāo

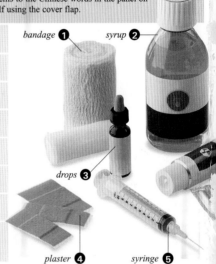

bandage **1**   *syrup* **2**

drops **3**

plaster **4**   *syringe* **5**

3 In conversation

你好，哪里不舒服？
Nǐhǎo, nǎli bù shūfu?

Hello. What's the matter?

我胃疼。
Wǒ wèi téng.

I have a stomachache.

你拉肚子吗？
Nǐ lādùzi ma?

Do you also have diarrhoea?

4 Words to remember

Familiarize yourself with these words and test yourself using the flap.

headache	头疼	tóu téng
stomachache	胃疼	wèi téng
diarrhoea	拉肚子	lādùzi
cold	感冒	gǎnmào
cough	咳嗽	késou
temperature	发烧	fāshāo
toothache	牙疼	yá téng

我头疼。
Wǒ tóu téng.
I have a headache.

6 Say it

I have a toothache.

I have a cough.

Do you you have that as an ointment?

8 ointment

7 suppository

6 tablets

5 Useful phrases

Learn these phrases and then test yourself using the cover flap.

I have a leg ache.	我腿疼。 Wǒ tuǐ téng.
Do you have that as a syrup?	这种药有糖浆型吗？ Zhè zhǒng yào yǒu tángjiāng xíng ma?
I'm allergic to penicillin.	我对青霉素过敏。 Wǒ duì qīngméisù guòmǐn.

我不拉肚子，但是头疼。
Wǒ bù lādùzi, dànshì tóu téng.

No I don't, but I have a headache.

吃这种药。
Chī zhèzhǒng yào.

Take this.

这种药有药片型吗？
Zhèzhǒng yào yǒu yàopiàn xíng ma?

Do you have that as tablets?

1 Warm up

Say " I have a toothache" and "I have leg ache." (pp.88–89)

Ask "What's the matter?" (pp.88–89)

身体部位 (shēntǐ bùwèi)
The body

Most parts of the body have more than one word used to refer to them in Chinese. For example, shoubi *(arm)* is also called gebo, and fu *(stomach)* is also called duzi. The words below are universally understood. Remember there is no plural, so yan is *eye* or *eyes* and jiao is *foot* or *feet*.

---

2 Match and repeat: body

Match the numbered parts of the body with the list on the left. Test yourself by using the cover flap.

1 手
shǒu

2 头
tóu

3 肩膀
jiānbǎng

4 肘
zhǒu

5 头发
tóufa

6 手臂
shǒubì

7 脖子
bózi

8 胸
xiōng

9 腹
fù

10 腿
tuǐ

11 膝
xī

12 脚
jiǎo

hand ❶
head ❷
shoulder ❸
❹ elbow
❺ hair
❻ arm
❼ neck
❽ chest
❾ stomach
❿ leg
⓫ knee
⓬ foot

1 Warm up

Say "I have a headache." (pp.88–89)

Now, say "I have an earache." (pp.90–91)

Ask "What's the matter?" (pp.88–89)

看医生 (kàn yīshēng)
With the doctor

Most Chinese doctors are badsed in hospitals rather than inseparate clinics. You will usually need to go to a hospital for an appointment, even for minor ailments. Many Chinese doctors speak good English, but you could need to give a basic explanation in Chinese, for example, to a receptionist.

2 Useful phrases you may hear

Learn these phrases and then test yourself using the cover flap to conceal the Chinese on the left.

不严重。 Bù yánzhòng.	*It's not serious.*
需要化验。 Xūyào huàyàn.	*Tests are needed.*
你骨折了。 Nǐ gǔzhé le.	*You have a fracture.*
你需要住院。 Nǐ xūyào zhùyuàn.	*You need to stay in hospital.*

你是不是在服药?
Nǐ shìbùshì zài fúyào?
Are you taking any medication?

3 In conversation

哪里不舒服?
Nǎli bù shūfu?

What's the matter?

我胸疼。
Wǒ xiōng téng.

I have a pain in my chest.

让我听听。
Ràng wǒ tīngting.

I'll need to examine you.

3 Match and repeat: face

Match the numbered facial features with the list on the right.

eye **1**

2 *eyebrow*

3 *nose*

4 *ear*

5 *mouth*

1	眼	yǎn
2	眉	méi
3	鼻子	bízi
4	耳朵	ěrduo
5	嘴	zuǐ

4 Useful phrases

Learn these phrases and then test yourself using the cover flap.

I have a backache.	我背疼。 Wǒ bèi téng.

I have a rash on my arm.	我手臂上有疹子。 Wǒ shǒubì shàng yǒu zhěnzi.

I don't feel well.	我感觉不舒服。 Wǒ gǎnjué bù shūfu.

5 Put into practice

Join in this conversation and test yourself using the cover flap.

哪里不舒服? Nǎli bù shūfu? *What's the matter?*	我感觉不舒服。 Wǒ gǎnjué bù shūfu.

Say: I don't feel well.

哪里疼? Nǎli téng? *Where does it hurt?*	我肩膀疼。 Wǒ jiānbǎng téng.

Say: I have an ache in my shoulder.

🇨🇳 **Cultural tip** There are separate emergency numbers in China depending on the service you require. Dial 110 for the police, 122 for ambulance, and 119 for fire service.

4 Useful phrases you may need to say

Learn these phrases and then test yourself using the cover flap.

I have diabetes.	我有糖尿病。 Wǒ yǒu tángniàobìng.
I have epilepsy.	我有癫痫症。 Wǒ yǒu diānxiánzhèng.
I have asthma.	我有哮喘。 Wǒ yǒu xiàochuǎn.
I have a heart condition.	我有心脏病。 Wǒ yǒu xīnzàngbìng.
I have a fever.	我发烧了。 Wǒ fāshāo le.
It's urgent.	我要看急诊。 Wǒ yào kàn jízhěn.
I feel breathless.	我感觉呼吸困难。 Wǒ gǎnjué hūxī kùnnán.

我怀孕了。
Wǒ huáiyùn le.
I'm pregnant.

5 Say it

I have a pain in my arm.

Is it urgent?

严重吗?
Yánzhòng ma?

Is it serious?

不严重。只是消化不良。
Bù yánzhòng. Zhǐshì xiāohuàbùliáng.

It's not serious. You only have indigestion.

噢，那我就放心了。
Ō, nà wǒ jiù fàngxīn le.

Oh! What a relief.

1 Warm up

Say "Where's the florist?" (pp.68–69)

Say "Tests are needed." (pp.92–93)

What is the Chinese for "mouth" and "head"? (pp.90–91)

在医院 (zài yīyuàn)
In hospital

It is useful to know a few basic Chinese phrases relating to hospitals for use in an emergency or in case you need to visit a friend or colleague in hospital. Chinese medical care is not always available to foreigners, so make sure you have adequate insurance.

2 Useful phrases

Familiarize yourself with these phrases. Conceal the Chinese with the cover flap and test yourself.

候诊室在哪里？ Hòuzhěnshì zài nǎli?	*Where's the waiting room?*
需要多久？ Xūyào duōjiǔ?	*How long does it take?*
疼吗？ Téng ma?	*Will it hurt?*
请躺在床上。 Qǐng tǎng zài chuáng shàng.	*Please lie down on the bed.*
六小时之内请不要吃东西。 Liù xiǎoshí zhǐnèi qǐng bùyào chī dōngxi.	*Please do not eat anything for six hours.*
头不要动。 Tóu bùyào dòng.	*Don't move your head.*
张开嘴。 Zhāngkāi zuǐ.	*Open your mouth.*
需要验血。 Xūyào yànxiě.	*A blood test is needed.*

护士
hùshi
nurse

你感觉好些吗？
Nǐ gǎnjué hǎoxiē ma?
Are you feeling better?

探望时间是几点钟？
Tànwàng shíjiān shì jǐ diǎnzhōng?
What are the visiting hours

3 Words to remember

Memorize these words and test yourself using the cover flap.

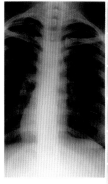

emergency ward	急诊室 jízhěnshì
children's ward	小儿病房 xiǎo'ér bìngfáng
operating theatre	手术室 shǒushùshì
waiting room	候诊室 hòuzhěnshì
corridor	走廊 zǒuláng
stairs	楼梯 lóutī
lift	电梯 diàntī

X光正常。
X-guāng zhèngcháng
The X-ray is normal.

4 Put into practice

Join in this conversation. Read the Chinese on the left and follow the instructions to make your reply. Then test yourself by hiding the answers with the cover flap.

不严重。
Bù yánzhòng.
It's not serious.

需要化验吗?
Xūyào huàyàn ma?

Ask: Are tests needed?

需要验血。
Xūyào yànxiě.
A blood test is needed.

疼吗?
Téng ma?

Ask: Will it hurt?

5 Say it

Is a blood test needed?

Where's the children's ward?

An X-ray is needed.

Read it The character for sickness is 病 bìng. So 病房 bìngfáng ("sickness room") is a ward, and 病人 bìngrén ("sick person") is a patient. It's also useful to be able to recognize the Chinese characters for hospital. This literally means "medical building": 医院 yīyuàn.

答案(dá'àn)
Answers
Cover with flap

复习与重温(fùxí yǔ chóngwēr
Review and repeat

1 The body

1 头
tóu

2 手臂
shǒubì

3 胸
xiōng

4 腹
fù

5 腿
tuǐ

6 膝
xī

7 脚
jiǎo

1 The body

Name the numbered body parts in Chinese.

- 1 head
- 2 arm
- chest 3
- 4 stomach
- leg 5
- knee 6
- foot 7

2 On the phone

1 请给我接王先生的电话。
Qǐng gěi wǒ jiē Wáng xiānsheng de diànhuà.

2 我是大通印刷厂的杰克·亨特。
Wǒ shì Dàtōng yìnshuāchǎng de Jiékè Hēngtè.

3 我可以给他留言吗?
Wǒ kěyǐ gěi tā liúyán ma?

4 会议不是星期四。
Huìyì bù shì xīngqīsì.

5 谢谢你。
Xièxie nǐ.

2 On the phone

You are arranging an appointment. Follow the conversation, replying in Chinese following the English prompts.

wei, wo shi zongji
1 *I'd like to speak to Mr Wang.*

nin shi shei ya
2 *I'm Jack Hunt of Tatong Printing.*

duibuqi, dianhua zhanxian
3 *Can I leave a message?*

dangran
4 *The meeting isn't on Tuesday.*

hen hao
5 *Thank you.*

答案(dá'àn)
Answers
Cover with flap

3 Clothing

Say the Chinese words for the numbered items of clothing.

jacket ❶

tie ❷

trousers ❸

shoes ❹

tights ❺

❻ *skirt*

3 Clothing

1 夹克衫
jiākèshān

2 领带
lǐngdài

3 裤子
kùzi

4 鞋
xié

5 裤袜
kùwà

6 裙子
qúnzi

4 At the doctor's

Say these phrases in Chinese.

1 *I have a pain in my leg.*

2 *Is it serious?*

3 *I have a heart condition.*

4 *Will it hurt?*

5 *I'm pregnant.*

4 At the doctor's

1 我腿疼。
Wǒ tuǐ téng.

2 严重吗?
Yánzhòng ma?

3 我有心脏病。
Wǒ yǒu
xīnzàngbìng.

4 疼吗?
Téng ma?

5 我怀孕了。
Wǒ huáiyùn le.

1 Warm up

Say the months of the year in Chinese. (pp.28–29)

Ask "Is there a museum nearby?" (pp.48–49) and "How much is that?" (pp.18–19)

家里(jiā lǐ)
Home

In the bigger Chinese cities, space is limited and most urban Chinese traditionally live in apartments (**gongyu**). More recently, however, affluent suburb shave sprung up on the outskirts accommodating successful entrepreneurs and business owners in large houses and Western-style estates.

2 Match and repeat

Match the numbered items to the list and test yourself using the flap.

1 天沟
  tiāngōu

2 阳台
  yángtái

3 窗户
  chuānghù

4 雨帘
  yǔlián

5 屋顶
  wūdǐng

6 墙
  qiáng

7 门
  mén

8 台阶
  táijiē

9 花园
  huāyuán

① *gutter*　　**②** *balcony*　　*window* **③**

garden **⑨**　　　　*steps* **⑧**　　*door* **⑦**

Cultural tip Features of buildings in China vary depending on the area, the climate, and the building materials available. In the north, heating is important, whereas in central and southern provinces, air-conditioning is a must. One almost universal feature is the presence of mosquito nets fixed on doors (shamen) and windows (shachuang).

3 Words to remember

Familiarize yourself with these words and test yourself using the flap.

room	房间	fángjiān
floor	地板	dìbǎn
ceiling	天花板	tiānhuābǎn
bedroom	卧室	wòshì
bathroom	卫生间	wèishēngjiān
kitchen	厨房	chúfáng
dining room	餐厅	cāntīng
living room	客厅	kètīng
attic	阁楼	gélóu
parking space	车库	chēkù

房租每月多少钱?
Fángzū měi yuè duōshao qián?
How much is the rent per month?

4 *canopy* **5** *roof*

6 *wall*

4 Useful phrases

Learn these phrases and test yourself.

有车库吗?
Yǒu chēkù ma?

Is there a parking space?

我什么时候能搬进来?
Wǒ shénme shíhou néng bān jìnlái?

When can I move in?

5 Say it

Is there a dining room?

Where's the kitchen?

It's furnished.

家具齐全吗?
Jiājù qíquán ma?

Is it furnished?

What's the Chinese for "table" (pp.20–21), "desk" (pp.80–81), "bed" (pp.60–61), and "curtains"? (pp.60–61)

How do you say "This car is small"? (pp.64–65)

屋内(wū nèi)
Inside the home

The Chinese often end their sentences with short "markers" that don't really change the meaning but carry different nuances. For example, the **yo** marker can imply *"and even"* or *"to be sure"* and **ne** can mean something like *"isn't that so?"* You'll see examples of these in the conversation below.

2 Match and repeat

Match the numbered items to the list in the panel on the left. Then test yourself by concealing the Chinese with the cover flap.

1 水池
  shuǐchí

2 水龙头
  shuǐlóngtóu

3 电饭煲
  diànfànbāo

4 厨台
  chútái

5 洗碗机
  xǐwǎnjī

6 椅子
  yǐzi

7 柜橱
  guìchú

8 桌子
  zhuōzi

2 *tap*
1 *sink*
5 *dishwasher* *chair* **6** *cabinet* **7** *table* **8**

3 In conversation

这是冰箱。
Zhè shì bīngxiāng.

This is the fridge.

有电饭煲吗?
Yǒu diànfànbāo ma?

Is there a rice cooker?

有。那是炉灶。
Yǒu. Nà shì lúzào.

Yes, there is. And here's the stove.

4 Words to remember

Familiarize yourself with these words and test yourself using the flap.

sofa	沙发	shāfā
carpet	地毯	dìtǎn
bath	浴缸	yùgāng
toilet	洗手间	xǐshǒujiān
stove	炉灶	lúzào
washing machine	洗衣机	xǐyījī
fridge	冰箱	bīngxiāng

沙发是新的呢。
Shāfā shì xīn de ne.
This sofa is new.

3 *rice cooker*
worktop **4**

5 Useful phrases

Learn these phrases and then test yourself using the cover flap to conceal the Chinese.

I'm not fond of the curtains.	我不喜欢这种窗帘。 Wǒ bù xǐhuān zhèzhǒng chuānglián.
The fridge is broken.	冰箱坏了。 Bīngxiāng huài le.
Are heat and electricity included?	包含供暖和供电吗？ Bāohán gōngnuǎn hé gōngdiàn ma?

6 Say it

Is there a washing machine?

The fridge is new.

The tap is broken.

水池是新的呢。
Shuǐchí shì xīn de ne.

The sink is new.

还有洗碗机呢。
Háiyǒu xǐwǎnjī ne.

And there's even a dishwasher.

瓷砖真好看哟。
Cízhuān zhēn hǎokàn yo.

What pretty tiles!

1 Warm up

What's the Chinese for "day" and "month"? (pp.28–29)

Say "Where's the florist?" (pp.68–69) and "Is there a garden?" (pp.98–99)

花园(huāyuán)
The garden

Chinese gardens, often with water features and plants like pine trees and bamboos, can be seen in public places such as parks, pagodas, and hotels. Space constraints mean that many Chinese homes don't have their own gardens, but house plants and flower arrangements are popular.

2 Words to remember

Familiarize yourself with these words and test yourself using the flap.

春 chūn	spring
夏 xià	summer
秋 qiū	autumn
冬 dōng	winter

pagoda **1**

tree **2**

stones **10**

pond **9**

rocks **8**

7 plants

3 Useful phrases

Learn these phrases and then test yourself using the cover flap.

	What kind of tree is this?	这是什么树？ Zhè shì shénme shù?
	I like the pond.	我喜欢这个池塘。 Wǒ xǐhuān zhège chítáng.
	What beautiful flowers!	花儿真好看。 Huār zhēn hǎokàn.
	Can we walk in the garden?	我们去花园散步，好吗？ Wǒmen qù huāyuán sànbù, hǎo ma?

4 Match and repeat

Match the numbered items to the words in the panel on the right.

3 *soil*

4 *flowers*

5 *grass*

path **6**

1 宝塔
  bǎotǎ

2 树
  shù

3 土
  tǔ

4 花儿
  huār

5 草
  cǎo

6 小路
  xiǎolù

7 植物
  zhíwù

8 岩石
  yánshí

9 池塘
  chítáng

10 石头
  shítou

5 Say it

What kind of flower is this?

I like the pagoda.

Is there a pond?

1 Warm up

Say "My name is John." (pp.8–9)

Say "I like the pond." (pp.102–103)

What's "fish" in Chinese? (pp.22–23)

动物(dòngwù)
Animals

The Chinese tend to keep small dogs such as Pekinese and sometimes cats in the house as pets. Birds and fish are also very popular. Keeping pets is generally becoming more popular, although official licences are required, which can be expensive.

2 Match and repeat

Match the numbered animals to the Chinese words in the panel on the left. Then test yourself using the cover flap.

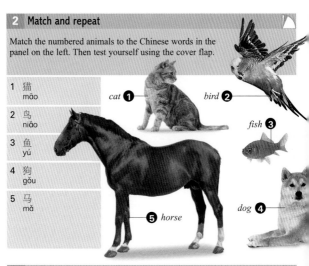

1 猫
  māo

2 鸟
  niǎo

3 鱼
  yú

4 狗
  gǒu

5 马
  mǎ

cat **1**

bird **2**

fish **3**

dog **4**

horse **5**

3 Useful phrases

Learn these phrases and then test yourself using the cover flap.

别担心，它很亲热人。 Bié dānxīn, tā hěn qīnrè rén.	*Don't worry. He's friendly.*
它叫什么名字？ Tā jiào shénme míngzi?	*What's his name?*
我不喜欢猫。 Wǒ bù xǐhuān māo.	*I'm not fond of cats.*
这狗不咬人。 Zhè gǒu bù yǎo rén.	*This dog doesn't bite.*

这是你家的猫吗？
Zhè shì nǐjiā de māo ma?
Is this your cat?

Cultural tip Some buildings and big houses will keep larger dogs outside, as guard dogs. These are known for their toughness and are treated as "yard" dogs rather than as pets. Look out for the "Beware of the dog" (xiaoxin you gou) sign.

---

4 Words to remember

Familiarize yourself with these words and test yourself using the flap.

monkey	猴	hóu
sheep	羊	yáng
cow	牛	niú
pig	猪	zhū
rabbit	兔	tù
tiger	虎	hǔ

这是什么鱼?
Zhè shì shénme yú?
*What kind of fish
is this?*

Read it Most basic words referring to natural features or animals, such as "tree", "dog", "flower", "cow", etc., are written with just a single character. Look at the characters for animals and natural features in week 10 and see if you can spot them in the phrases.

---

5 Put into practice

Join in this conversation. Read the Chinese on the left and follow the instructions to make your reply. Then test yourself by concealing the answers with the cover flap.

这是你家的狗吗?
Zhè shì nǐjiā de gǒu ma?
Is this your dog?

Say: Yes, his name
is Guoguo.

是的。它的名字叫
果果。
Shì de .Tā de míngzi jiào
guǒguo.

我不喜欢狗。
Wǒ bù xǐhuān gǒu.
I'm not fond of dogs.

Say: Don't worry. He's
friendly.

别担心, 它很亲热人。
Bié dānxīn,tā hěn
qīnrè rén.

答案(dá'àn)
Answers
Cover with flap

复习与重温(fùxí yǔ chóngwēn)
Review and repeat

---

1 Colours

1 白
bái

2 黄
huáng

3 绿
lǜ

4 黑
hēi

5 红
hóng

6 蓝
lán

7 粉红
fěnhóng

1 Colours

What are these colours in Chinese?

1 *white*   5 *red*

2 *yellow*   6 *blue*

3 *green*   7 *pink*

4 *black*

---

2 Kitchen

1 厨台
chútái

2 水池
shuǐchí

3 水龙头
shuǐlóngtóu

4 电饭煲
diànfànbāo

5 洗碗机
xǐwǎnjī

6 椅子
yǐzi

7 柜橱
guìchú

8 桌子
zhuōzi

2 Kitchen

Say the Chinese words for the numbered items.

1 *worktop*   *sink* **2**   **3** *tap*

dishwasher **5**   *chair* **6**   *cabinet* **7**

答案(dá'àn)
Answers
Cover with flap

3 House

You are visiting a house in China. Join in the conversation, replying in Chinese where you see the English prompts.

zhe shi weishengjian
1 *What pretty tiles!*

zhe shi guanxishi
2 *Is there a washing machine?*

you xiyiji
3 *Is there a parking space?*

mei you cheku. you huayuan
4 *Is it furnished?*

jiaju qiquan
5 *How much is the rent per month?*

3 House

1 瓷砖真好看哟.
   Cízhuān zhēn hǎokàn yo.

2 有洗衣机吗?
   Yǒu xǐyījī ma?

3 有车库吗?
   Yǒu chēkù ma?

4 家具齐全吗?
   Jiājù qíquán ma?

5 房租每月多少钱?
   Fángzū měiyuè duōshao qián?

④ rice cooker

⑧ table

4 At home

Say the Chinese for the following items.

1 *washing machine*
2 *sofa*
3 *attic*
4 *dining room*
5 *tree*
6 *garden*

4 At home

1 洗衣机
   xǐyījī

2 沙发
   shāfā

3 阁楼
   gélóu

4 餐厅
   cāntīng

5 树
   shù

6 花园
   huāyuán

1 Warm up

Ask "How do I get to the station?", and "Where's the post office?" (pp.50–51 and pp.68–69)

What's the Chinese for "passport"? (pp.54–55)

Ask "What time is it?" (pp.30–31)

邮局和银行
(yóujú hé yínháng)
Post office and bank

Post office signs or buildings and postboxes are painted green in China. Most banks are open for business on Sundays. Only the Bank of China handles currency exchange and their ATMs allow foreign bank cards to withdraw Chinese currency (**Renminbi**) up to certain limits.

2 Words to remember: post

Familiarize yourself with these words and test yourself using the cover flap to conceal the Chinese on the left.

邮局 yóujú	post office
信件 xìnjiàn	letter
信封 xìnfēng	envelope
邮包 yóubāo	parcel
航空邮件 hángkōng yóujiàn	air mail
邮票 yóupiào	stamps
邮递员 yóudìyuán	postman
邮箱 yóuxiāng	postbox

明信片
míngxìnpiàn
postcard

3 In conversation

请给我兑换旅行支票，好吗？
Qǐng gěi wǒ duìhuàn lǚxíngzhīpiào, hǎo ma?

I'd like to change some traveller's cheques.

您有身份证吗？
Nín yǒu shēnfènzhèng ma?

Do you have any identification?

有。这是我的护照。
Yǒu. Zhè shì wǒ de hùzhào.

Yes, I do. Here's my passport.

4 Words to remember: bank

Familiarize yourself with these words and test yourself using the cover flap to conceal the Chinese on the right.

信用卡
xìnyòngkǎ
credit card

我能用信用卡付款吗?
Wǒ néng yòng xìnyòngkǎ
fùkuǎn ma?
Can I pay with a credit card?

bank	银行	yínháng
money	钱	qián
traveller's cheques	旅行支票	lǚxíngzhīpiào
banknotes	纸币	zhǐbì
coins	硬币	yìngbì
cash point	自动提款机	zìdòng tíkuǎnjī
exchange rate	汇率	huìlǜ

5 Useful phrases

Learn these phrases and then test yourself using the cover flap.

6 Say it

I'd like to change some dollars.

Here's my credit card.

Where's the postbox?

I'd like to change some money, please. 请给我换点钱, 好吗?
Qǐng gěi wǒ huàndiǎn qián, hǎo ma?

What is the exchange rate? 汇率是多少?
Huìlǜ shì duōshao?

Where's the cash point? 哪里有自动提款机?
Nǎli yǒu zìdòng tíkuǎnjī?

请在这里签字。
Qǐng zài zhèli qiānzì.

Please *sign here*.

您要多大面值的纸币?
Nín yào duōdà miànzhí de zhǐbì?

How would you like the notes?

请给我100元面值的。
Qǐng gěi wǒ yībǎi yuán miànzhí de.

I'd like 100-yuan notes, please.

1 Warm up

What is the Chinese for "The fridge is broken"? (pp.100–101)

What's the Chinese for "today" and "tomorrow"? (pp.28–29)

Say "Thank you." (pp. 40–41)

修理(xiūlǐ)
Repairs

You can combine the Chinese words on these pages with the vocabulary you learned in week 10 to help you explain basic problems and cope with arranging most repairs. Rented accommodation is usually arranged via agents, known as **zufang zhongjie**. They can also help with problems.

2 Words to remember

Familiarize yourself with these words and test yourself using the flap.

管道工 guǎndàogōng	*plumber*
电工 diàngōng	*electrician*
机械师 jīxièshī	*mechanic*
修理工 xiūlǐgōng	*handyman*
木匠 mùjiang	*carpenter*
电脑修理店 diànnǎo xiūlǐdiàn	*computer repair shop*
清洁工 qīngjiégōng	*cleaner*
厨师 chúshī	*cook*

我想请一名机械师。
Wǒ xiǎng qǐng yī míng jīxièshī.
I need a mechanic.

3 In conversation

早上好。我是韩红。
Zǎoshang hǎo. Wǒ shì Hán Hóng.

Good morning. This is Han Hong.

早上好。有什么问题吗?
Zǎoshang hǎo. Yǒu shénme wèntí ma?

Good morning. Is there a problem?

洗碗机坏了。
Xǐwǎnjī huài le.

The dishwasher is broken.

4 Useful phrases

Learn these phrases and then test yourself using the cover flap.

Please clean the room.

请整理房间吧。
Qǐng zhěnglǐ fángjiān ba.

Can you repair the television?

你能修理电视机吗?
Nǐ néng xiūlǐ diànshìjī ma?

Can you recommend a good handyman?

你能推荐一个好的修理工吗?
Nǐ néng tuījiàn yī gè hǎo de xiūlǐgōng ma?

哪里才能修理它呢?
Nǎli cáinéng xiūlǐ tā ne?
Where can I get this repaired?

5 Put into practice

Cover up the text on the right and complete the dialogue in Chinese.

您的光驱坏了。
Nín de guāngqū huài le.
Your CD drive is broken.

你能推荐一个好的电脑修理店吗?
Nǐ néng tuījiàn yī gè hǎo de diànnǎo xiūlǐdiàn ma?

Ask: Can you recommend a good computer repair shop?

街上有一家。
Jiēshàng yǒu yìjiā.
There's one in the town.

谢谢你。
Xièxie nǐ.

今天能修理。
Jīntiān néng xiūlǐ.
It's possible to repair it today.

Say: Thank you.

我们会派一名修理工去。
Wǒmen huìpài yī míng xiūlǐgōng qù.

We'll send a handyman.

今天就派, 好吗?
Jīntiān jiù pài, hǎo ma?

Can you do it today, please?

对不起。明天上午派。
Duìbuqǐ. Míngtiān shàngwǔ pài.

Sorry. But it will be tomorrow morning.

Say the days of the week in Chinese. (pp.28–29)

How do you say "cleaner"? (pp.110–111)

Say "It's 9.30", "10.45", and "12.00." (pp.30–31)

来(lái)
To come

Chinese verbs generally do not change with the subject (I,you, he, she, we, they). Sometimes, however, these verbs need to be followed by time-indicating characters. Below, you will see some of these changes for the verb 来 **lai** *(to come)*.

2   Useful phrases

Say the different forms of **lai** *(to come)* aloud. Use the cover flap to test yourself and, when you are confident, practise the sample sentences below.

来 lái	*to come* *(infinitive)*
来了 lái le	*come/coming* *(present)*
不来了 bù lái le	*not come/coming* *(present negative)*
来过 láiguò	*came* *(past)*
没来过 méi láiguò	*didn't come* *(past negative)*
来吧! Lái ba!	*Please come!* *(invitation)*
公共汽车来了。 Gōnggòng qìchē lái le.	*The bus is coming.*
木匠九点钟来过。 Mùjiang jiǔ diǎnzhōng láiguò.	*The carpenter came* *at nine o'clock.*
清洁工今天没来过。 Qīngjiégōng jīntiān méi láiguò.	*The cleaner didn't* *come today.*
我明天来。 Wǒ míngtiān lái.	*I'll come tomorrow.*

他们乘火车来。
Tāmen chéng huǒchē lái.
They're coming
by train.

■ **Conversational tip** Beware of English phrases using "come" that translate differently in Chinese. For example, the Chinese equivalent of "I come from Canada" would be "wo shi Jianadaren", which translates literally as " I am Canada person".

3 Invitations

You can use **lai** (*come*) for invitations. There are different expressions depending on the level of formality.

请来参加我的生日晚会吧。
Qǐng lái cānjiā wǒ de shēngrì wǎnhuì ba.

Please come to join my birthday party.

星期一您能不能来我们的接待室?
Xīngqīyī nín néngbùnéng lái wǒmen de jiēdàishì?

On Monday, can you come to our reception? (formal)

星期五您能不能来参加我们的座谈会?
Xīngqīwǔ nín néngbùnéng lái cānjiā wǒmen de zuòtánhuì?

On Friday, can you come to join our seminar? (formal)

来参加我的晚宴吧!
Lái cānjiā wǒ de wǎnyàn ba!

Come to my dinner party! (informal)

4 Put into practice

Join in this conversation. Read the Chinese on the left and follow the instructions to make your reply. Then test yourself by concealing the answers with the cover flap.

喂, 你好。
Wèi, nǐhǎo.
Hello.

Say: Hello. Please come to join my birthday party.

你好。请来参加我的生日晚会吧。
Nǐhǎo. Qǐng lái cānjiā wǒ de shēngrì wǎnhuì ba.

晚会什么时候开始?
Wǎnhuì shénme shíhou kāishǐ?
What time does the party begin?

Say: Eight o'clock, tomorrow evening.

明天晚上8点。
Míngtiān wǎnshang bā diǎn.

好。我一定来。
Hǎo. Wǒ yīdìng lái.
Yes, I'd love to come.

Say: See you tomorrow.

明天见。
Míngtiān jiàn.

What's the Chinese for "tall" and "short"? (pp.64–65)

Say "The room is big" and "The bed is small." (pp.64–65)

警察与犯罪
(jǐngchá yǔ fànzuì)
Police and crime

Chinese police cars have the two characters 公安 **gong'an** (*public security*) or 交警 **jiaojing** (*traffic police*) displayed. Note that the terms **nanren** (*man*) and **nüren** (*woman*) in section 4 are not very polite as they refer to criminal suspects. More polite equivalents would be **nanshi** and **nüshi**.

2 Words to remember: crime

Familiarize yourself with these words.

扒手 **páshǒu**	*thief/burglar*
警方报告 **jǐngfāng bàogào**	*police report*
证词 **zhèngcí**	*statement*
证人 **zhèngrén**	*witness*
目击者 **mùjīzhě**	*eye-witness*
律师 **lùshī**	*lawyer*
警官 **jǐngguān**	*police officer*

我需要请律师。
Wǒ xūyào qǐng lùshī.
I need a lawyer.

3 Useful phrases

Learn these phrases and then test yourself using the cover flap.

我的手袋被偷了。 **Wǒ de shǒudài bèi tōu le.**	*I've been pick-pocketed.*	照相机 **zhàoxiàngjī** *camera*
丢失了什么? **Diūshī le shénme?**	*What was stolen?*	
你看见是谁偷的吗? **Nǐ kànjiàn shì shuí tōu de ma?**	*Did you see who did it?*	钱 **qián** *money*
什么时候发生的? **Shénme shíhou fā shēng de?**	*When did it happen?*	钱包 **qiánbāo** *wallet*

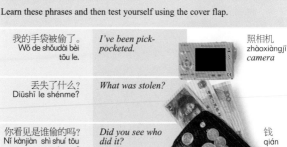

4 Words to remember: appearance

Learn these words and then test yourself using the cover flap.

那男人棕色头发, 戴眼镜。
Nà nánrén zōngsè tóufa,
dài yǎnjìng.
*The man had brown hair
and glasses.*

那女人很高, 长头发。
Nà nǚrén hěn gāo, cháng
tóufa.
*The woman was tall and
had long hair.*

man/men	男人	nánrén
woman/women	女人	nǚrén
tall	高	gāo
short	矮	ǎi
young	青年	qīngnián
middle-aged	中年	zhōngnián
fat	胖	pàng
thin	瘦	shòu
with a beard	有络腮胡子	yǒu luòsāi-húzi
with a moustache	有小胡子	yǒu xiǎohúzi
wearing glasses	戴眼镜	dàiyǎnjing

Read it The Chinese for "police" is written with two characters: 警察 (jingcha). Changing the last of these characters to 官 (guan) will produce "police officer": 警官 (jingguan); and adding the character 局 (ju) will produce the word for "police station": 警察局 (jingchaju).

5 Put into practice

Practise these phrases. Then use the cover flap to hide the text on the right and follow the instructions to make your reply in Chinese.

他长得什么样?
Tā zhǎng de shénme-
yàng?
Can you describe him?

Say: The man was
short.

那男人很矮。
Nà nánrén hěn ǎi.

头发呢?
Tóufa ne?
And the hair?

Say: Brown hair with
a beard.

棕色头发, 有络腮
胡子。
Zōngsè tóufa, yǒu
luòsāi-húzi.

答案(dá'àn)
Answers
Cover with flap

复习与重温(fùxí yǔ chóngwēn)
Review and repeat

1 To come

1 我乘公共汽车来。
Wǒ chéng gōnggòng qìchē lái.

2 昨天电工来过。
Zuótiān diàngōng láiguò.

3 请来参加我的生日晚会。
Qǐng lái cānjiā wǒ de shēngrì wǎnhuì.

4 星期四清洁工没来过。
Xīngqīsì qīngjiégōng méi láiguò.

1 To come

Put the following sentences into Chinese using the correct form of **lai** (*to come*).

1 *I'm coming by bus.*

2 *The electrician came yesterday.*

3 *Please come and join my birthday party.*

4 *The cleaner didn't come on Thursday.*

2 Bank and post

1 信用卡
xìnyòngkǎ

2 纸币
zhǐbì

3 明信片
míngxìnpiàn

4 信封
xìnfēng

5 邮票
yóupiào

2 Bank and post

Name the numbered items in Chinese.

credit card ❶

❷ *banknotes*

❸ *postcard*

❹ *envelope*

❺ *stamps*

答案(dá'àn)
Answers
Cover with flap

3 Appearance

What do these descriptions mean?

1 ta shi aigezi, yeshi shouzi

2 na nanren shi duantoufa

3 na nüren dai yanjing

4 na nanren you
xiaohuzi

5 ta toufa huabai,
you luosaihuzi

3 Appearance

1 *He/She was short
and thin.*

2 *The man had
short hair.*

3 *The woman
wears glasses.*

4 *The man had
a moustache.*

5 *He had grey hair
with a beard.*

4 The pharmacy

You are asking a pharmacist for advice. Join in
the conversation, replying in Chinese where you
see the English prompts.

nihao, nali bu shufu
1 *I have a stomachache.*

ni laduzi ma
2 *No, but I have a headache.*

chi zhezhong yao
3 *Do you have that as a syrup?*

you
4 *How much is that?*

wushi yuan
5 *Thank you.*

4 The pharmacy

1 我胃疼。
Wǒ wèi téng.

2 不。我头疼。
Bù. Wǒ tóu téng.

3 这种药有糖浆型
吗?
Zhèzhǒng yào yǒu
tángjiāng xíng ma?

4 多少钱?
Duōshao qián?

5 谢谢。
Xièxie.

1 Warm up

What is the Chinese for "museum" and "cinema?" (pp.48–49)

Say "I like the pond." (pp.102–103)

Ask "What's your profession?" (pp.78–79)

休闲娱乐(xiūxián yúlè)
Leisure time

Popular leisure activities outside the house include shopping and going to karaoke bars, and going to the cinema. **Puke** (*cards*), **majiang** (*mahjong*), **xiangqi** (*Chinese chess*), and other traditional games are popular with older people, while theatre and opera are only minority pursuits.

2 Words to remember

Familiarize yourself with these words and test yourself using the cover flap to conceal the Chinese on the left.

剧场 jùchǎng	*theatre*
看电影 kàn diànyǐng	*watching films*
主题公园 zhǔtí gōngyuán	*theme park*
音乐 yīnyuè	*music*
艺术 yìshù	*art*
运动 yùndòng	*sport*
旅游 lǚyóu	*travelling*
读书 dúshū	*reading*

我喜欢看京剧。
Wǒ xǐhuān kàn jīngjù.
I like Chinese opera.

演员
yǎnyuán
actor

3 In conversation

你想去卡拉ok厅吗?
Nǐ xiǎng qù kǎlā-OK tīng ma?

Do you want to go to a karaoke bar?

我并不喜欢卡拉ok。
Wǒ bìng bù xǐhuān kǎlā-OK.

I don't really like karaoke.

你业余时间做什么?
Nǐ yèyú shíjiān zuò shénme?

What do you do in your free time?

4 Useful phrases

Learn these phrases and then test yourself using the cover flap.

我喜欢玩电子游戏。
Wǒ xǐhuān wán diànzǐ yóuxì.
I like video games.

布景
bùjǐng
set

What do you do in your free time? (formal)	您业余时间做什么? Nín yèyú shíjiān zuò shénme?
What do you do in your free time? (informal).	你业余时间做什么? Nǐ yèyú shíjiān zuò shénme?
My hobby is reading.	我的爱好是读书。 Wǒ de àihào shì dúshū.
I like watching films.	我喜欢看电影。 Wǒ xǐhuān kàn diànyǐng.
I hate shopping.	我最不喜欢购物了。 Wǒ zuì bù xǐhuān gòuwù le.

舞台
wǔtái
stage

5 Say it

I like music.

I don't really like watching films.

My hobby is opera.

I hate theme parks.

我喜欢购物。
Wǒ xǐhuān gòuwù.

I like shopping.

我最不喜欢购物了。
Wǒ zuì bù xǐhuān gòuwù le.

I hate shopping.

没问题。我自己去。
Méi wèntí. Wǒ zìjǐ qù.

No problem, I'll go on my own.

1 Warm up

What's the Chinese for "fish"? (pp.104–105)

Say "I like the theatre" and "I like travelling." (pp.118–119)

Say "I don't really like…" (pp.118–119)

运动与爱好
(yùndòng yǔ àihào)
Sport and hobbies

Traditional Chinese sports, which are still popular, include martial arts **xiangqi**, Chinese wrestling **weiqi (go)**, and dragon-boat racing. Basketball, table tennis, badminton, football, and golf have also established themselves. Arts and crafts include embroidery, paper-cutting, and calligraphy.

2 Words to remember

Memorize these words and then test yourself.

足球 zúqiú	*football*
篮球 lánqiú	*basketball*
乒乓 pīngpāng	*table tennis*
游泳 yóuyǒng	*swimming*
登山 dēngshān	*mountain climbing*
钓鱼 diàoyú	*fishing*
画画 huàhuà	*painting*
书法 shūfǎ	*calligraphy*

沙坑
shākēng
bunker

高尔夫球手
gāo'ěrfúqiú-
shǒu
golfer

我每天打高尔夫。
Wǒ měitiān dǎ gāo'ěrfú.
I play golf every day.

3 Useful phrases

Familiarize yourself with these phrases.

我打棒球。 Wǒ dǎ bàngqiú.	*I play baseball.*
他打乒乓。 Tā dǎ pīngpāng.	*He plays table tennis.*
她喜欢画画。 Tā xǐhuān huàhuà.	*She likes painting.*

4 Phrases to remember

Learn the phrases below and then test yourself. Notice that "play" is **da** or **ti** (literally "kick") for sports, but **la** for musical instruments.

我拉小提琴。
wǒ lā xiǎotíqín.
I play the violin.

旗子
qízi
flag

高尔夫球场
gāo'ěrfūqiúchǎng
golf course

What do you like doing? (formal)	您想做什么？ Nín xiǎng zuò shénme?
What do you like doing? (informal)	你想玩儿什么？ Nǐ xiǎng wánr shénme?
I like playing golf.	我想打高尔夫。 Wǒ xiǎng dǎ gāo'ěrfū.
I like playing table tennis.	我想打乒乓。 Wǒ xiǎng dǎ pīngpāng.
I play football.	我踢足球。 Wǒ tī zúqiú.
I like going fishing.	我想去钓鱼。 Wǒ xiǎng qù diàoyú.
I go mountain climbing.	我去登山。 Wǒ qù dēngshān.

5 Put into practice

Learn these phrases. Then cover up the text on the right and complete the dialogue in Chinese. Check your answers.

你想玩儿什么？
Nǐ xiǎng wánr shénme.
What do you like doing?

Say: I like playing football.

我想踢足球。
Wǒ xiǎng tī zúqiú.

你打篮球吗？
Nǐ dǎ lánqiú ma?
Do you play basketball?

Say: No, I play golf.

不。我打高尔夫。
Bù. Wǒ dǎ gāo'ěrfū.

你经常打吗？
Nǐ jīngcháng dǎ ma?
Do you play often?

Say: Every week.

每星期打一次。
Měi xīngqī dǎ yī cì.

Say "your husband" and "your wife." (pp.12–13)

How do you say "lunch" and "dinner" in Chinese? (pp.20–21)

Say "Sorry, I'm busy that day." (pp.32–33)

社交(shèjiāo)
Socializing

As a business guest, it's more common to be invited to a restaurant than to someone's home. This is partly practical—people often have long commutes. But if you're staying for longer, you may be invited for a meal or a party.

2 Useful phrases

Learn these phrases and then test yourself.

您想来参加晚宴吗？ Nín xiǎng lái cānjiā wǎnyàn ma?	*Would you like to come for dinner?*
星期三怎么样？ Xīngqīsān zěnmeyàng?	*What about Wednesday?*
下一次吧。 Xiàyīcì ba.	*Perhaps another time.*

Cultural tip When visiting a Chinese home, remember that it's usual to remove your outdoor shoes at the door. Take a gift for the host or hostess. Flowers, a bottle of drink, or a present from your home country will be greatly appreciated.

3 In conversation

您想来参加星期二的晚宴吗？
Nín xiǎng lái cānjiā xīngqī'èr de wǎnyàn ma?

Would you like to come for dinner on Tuesday?

对不起，我星期二很忙。
Duìbuqǐ, wǒ xīngqī'èr hěn máng.

Sorry. I'm busy on Tuesday.

星期四怎么样？
Xīngqīsì zěnmeyàng?

What about Thursday?

4 Words to remember

Familiarize yourself with these words and test yourself using the flap.

客人
kèrén
guest

东道主
dōngdàozhǔ
host

party	晚会 wǎnhuì	
invitation	邀请 yāoqǐng	
gift	礼物 lǐwù	

Read it You now know the principle of how the Chinese script works and can recognize some basic recurring characters. You'll also find more information on pp.152–157 to further expand your understanding.

5 Put into practice

Join in this conversation.

我们星期日有一个晚会。你能来吗?
Wǒmen xīngqìrì yǒu yī gè wǎnhuì. Nǐ néng lái ma?
We are having a party on Sunday. Are you free to come?
Say: Yes, how nice!

好,那太好了。
Hǎo, nà tài hǎo le.

那太好了。
Nà tài hǎo le.
That's great!

Say: At what time should we arrive?

我们几点钟来呢?
Wǒmen jǐ diǎnzhōng lái ne?

谢谢你的邀请。
Xièxie nǐ de yāoqǐng.
Thank you for inviting us.

好,那太好了。
Hǎo, nà tài hǎo le.

Yes, how nice!

请带你的先生一起来。
Qǐng dài nǐ de xiānsheng yīqǐ lái.

Please bring your husband.

我们几点钟来呢?
Wǒmen jǐ diǎnzhōng lái ne?

At what time should we come?

答案(dá'àn)
Answers
Cover with flap

复习与重温(fùxí yǔ chóngwēn)
Review and repeat

1 Animals

1 猫
mão

2 鸟
niǎo

3 马
mǎ

4 鱼
yú

5 狗
gǒu

1 Animals

Name the numbered animals in Chinese.

1 cat

bird **2**

4 fish

2 I like...

1 我想打棒球。
Wǒ xiǎng dǎ
bàngqiú.

2 我想打高尔夫。
Wǒ xiǎng dǎ
gāo'ěrfū

3 我想画画。
Wǒ xiǎng huàhuà.

2 I like...

Say the following in Chinese:

1 *I like playing baseball.*

2 *I like playing golf.*

3 *I like painting.*

❸ *horse*

❺ *dog*

答案(dá'àn)
Answers

Cover with flap

3 Leisure

What do these Chinese sentences mean?

1 wo zui bu xihuan kala-OK

2 wo xihuan wan dianzi youxi

3 wo de aihao shi dushu

4 wo bing bu xihuan gouwu

5 wo la xiaotiqin

3 Leisure

1 *I hate karaoke.*

2 *I like video games.*

3 *My hobby is reading.*

4 *I don't really like shopping.*

5 *I play the violin.*

4 An invitation

You are invited for dinner. Join in the conversation, replying in Chinese following the English prompts.

nin xiang lai canjia xingqiliu de wanyan ma
1 *Sorry, I'm busy on Saturday.*

xingqisi zenmeyang
2 *Yes, how nice!*

qing dai ni de xiansheng yiqi lai
3 *At what time should we arrive?*

wanshang ba dian
4 *Thank you very much.*

4 An invitation

1 对不起，我星期 六很忙。
Duìbuqǐ, wǒ xīngqīliù hěn máng.

2 好，那太好了
Hǎo, nà tài hǎo le.

3 我们几点钟来 呢?
Wǒmen jǐ diǎnzhōng lái ne?

4 谢谢你。
Xièxie nǐ.

Reinforce and progress

Regular practice is the key to maintaining and advancing your language skills. In this section, you will find a variety of suggestions for reinforcing and extending your knowledge of Chinese. Many involve returning to exercises in the book and using the dictionary to extend their scope. Go back through the lessons in a different order, mix and match activities to make up your own 15-minute daily programme, or focus on topics that are of particular relevance to your current needs.

Keep warmed up
Re-visit the Warm Up boxes to remind yourself of key words and phrases. Make sure you work your way through all of them on a regular basis.

1 Warm up

Ask "How much is that?" (pp.18–19)

What are "breakfast", "lunch", and "dinner"? (pp.20–21)

What are "three", "four", "five", and "six"? (pp.10–11)

2 I'd like...

Say you'd like the following:

cake **1**

2 tea

3 coffee

4 sugar

Review and repeat again
Work through a Review and Repeat lesson as a way of reinforcing words and phrases presented in the course. Return to the main lesson for any topic on which you are no longer confident.

3 In conversation: taxi

Carry on conversing
Re-read the In Conversation panels. Say both parts of the conversation, paying attention to the pronunciation. Where possible, try incorporating new words from the dictionary.

请带我去故宫。
Qǐng dài wǒ qù Gùgōng.

I'd like to go to the Forbidden City, please

上车吧。
Shàngchē ba.

Do get in.

我就在这儿下车，以吗？
Wǒ jiùzài zhèr xiàch kěyǐ ma?

Can you drop me please?

4 Useful phrases

Learn these phrases and then test yourself using the flap.

营业	*What time do you open?*	你们什么时间开门？ Nǐmen shénme shíjiān kāimén?
	What time do you close?	你们什么时间关门？ Nǐmen shénme shíjiān guānmén?
Smart Identity Card Centre 智能身份證中心	*Is wheelchair access possible?*	轮椅可以方便进出吗？ Lúnyǐ kěyǐ fāngbiàn jìnchū ma?

Practise phrases
Return to the Useful Phrases and Put into Practice exercises. Test yourself using the cover flap. When you are confident, devise your own versions of the phrases, using new words from the dictionary.

Match, repeat, and extend
Remind yourself of words related to specific topics by returning to the Match and Repeat and Words to Remember exercises. Test yourself using the cover flap. Discover new words in that area by referring to the dictionary and menu guide.

3 Match and repeat

Match the numbered items to the Chinese words in the panel on the left and test yourself using the cover flap.

鼠标
shǔbiāo

适配器
shìpèiqì

变压器
biànyāqì

笔记本电脑
bǐjìběn diànnǎo

屏幕
píngmù

保修证
bǎoxiūzhèng

内存
nèicún

电池
diànchí

4 laptop

5 screen

1 mouse

2 adapter

3 transformer

8 battery

7 memory

6 guarantee

6 Say it
What kind of flower is this?

I like the waterfall.

Is there a pond?

Say it again
The Say It exercises are a useful instant reminder for each lesson. Practise these, using your own vocabulary variations from the dictionary or elsewhere in the lesson.

Using other resources

In addition to working with this book, try the following language extension ideas:

• Visit China if you can and try out your new skills with native speakers. Otherwise, find out if there is a Mandarin-speaking community near you. There may be shops, cafés, restaurants, and clubs. Try to visit some of these and use your Chinese to order food and drink and strike up conversations. Most native speakers will be happy to speak Chinese to you.

• Join a language class or club. There are usually evening and day classes available at a variety of different levels. Or you could start a club yourself if you have friends who are also interested in keeping up their Chinese.

• Practise your new knowledge of the Chinese characters (see pp.152–157). Look at the back of food packages and other products. You will often find a Chinese list of ingredients or components. See if you can spot some familiar characters in the Chinese list and then compare to the English equivalent.

• Look at the titles and advertisements of Chinese magazines and comics. The pictures will help you to decipher the script. Look for familiar words and characters, even if you can't make out the whole text.

• Use the internet to find websites for learning languages, some of which offer free online help.

Menu guide

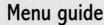

This guide lists the most common terms you may encounter on Chinese menus. Dishes are divided into categories and the Chinese script is displayed clearly to help you identify items on a menu.

Rice and noodle dishes

miàntiáo	面条	*noodles*
mǐfàn	米饭	*rice*
nuòmǐ	糯米	*glutinous rice*
chǎofàn	炒饭	*fried rice*
dàn chǎofàn	蛋炒饭	*fried rice with egg*
chǎomiàn	炒面	*fried noodles*
chǎo mǐfěn	炒米粉	*fried rice noodles*
zhōu	粥	*rice porridge*

Basic food items

chūnjuǎn	春卷	*spring rolls*
dòushābāo	豆沙包	*steamed dumplings with sweet bean paste filling*
huājuǎn	花卷	*steamed rolls*
mántou	馒头	*steamed bread*

miànbāo	面包	*bread* (white)
nǎilào	奶酪	*cheese*
ròu	肉	*meat* (usually pork)
xiáncài	咸菜	*pickles*

Cooking methods and combinations

chǎo...	炒……	*stir-fried...*
chāshāo...	叉烧……	*barbecued...*
...dīng	……丁	*diced...*
dōnggū...	冬菇……	*...with dried mushrooms*
gālí...	咖喱……	*curried...*
gōngbǎo...	宫保……	*stir-fried... with peanuts and chilli*
háoyóu...	蚝油……	*...with oyster sauce*
hóngshāo...	红烧……	*...braised in brown sauce*
huáliū...	滑溜……	*stir-fried ...with sauce added*
huì...	烩……	*stewed...*
huǒguō...	火锅……	*...in hotpot*
huǒtuǐ...	火腿……	*...with ham*
jiācháng...	家常……	*home-style...*
kǎo...	烤……	*roasted...*

...kuài	·····块	*...chunks, pieces*
làzi...	辣子·····	*...with chilli*
májiàng...	麻酱·····	*...quick-fried in sesame paste*
málà...	麻辣·····	*...with chilli and wild pepper*
...piàn	·····片	*sliced...*
fānqiézhī...	番茄汁·····	*...with tomato sauce*
qīngzhēng...	清蒸·····	*steamed...*
sānxiān...	三鲜·····	*"three-fresh" ... (with three varied ingredients)*
...sī	·····丝	*shredded...*
tángcù ...wán	糖醋·····丸	*sweet and sour... balls*
xiāngsū...	香酥·····	*crispy deep-fried...*
zhá...	炸·····	*deep-fried...*
zhàcài...	榨菜·····	*...with pickled mustard greens*
zhēng...	蒸 ·····	*steamed...*

Pork

zhūròu	猪肉	*pork*
chāshāoròu	叉烧肉	*barbecued pork*
fěnzhēngròu	粉蒸肉	*steamed pork with rice*

làzi ròudīng	辣子肉丁	*stir-fried diced pork with chilli*
mùxū ròu	木须肉	*stir-fried sliced pork with eggs, tree-ear (edible fungus), and day lily (type of dried lily)qīng*
qīngjiāo chǎo ròupiàn	青椒炒肉片	*stir-fried sliced pork roupian with pepper*
sǔn chǎo ròupiàn	笋炒肉片	*stir-fried sliced pork with bamboo shoots*
tángcù páigǔ	糖醋排骨	*spare ribs cooked in a sweet and sour sauce*
zhàcài ròusī	榨菜肉丝	*stir-fried shredded pork with pickled mustard greens*

Chicken and duck

jī	鸡	*chicken*
jīdīng	鸡丁	*diced chicken*
jiàng bào jīdīng	酱爆鸡丁	*diced chicken quick-fried with bean sauce*
báizhǎnjī	白斩鸡	*sliced cold chicken*
jiàohuājī	叫化鸡	*"beggar's chicken" (charcoal-baked marinaded chicken)*
yā	鸭	*duck*
Běijīng kǎoyā	北京烤鸭	*Peking roast duck*
xiānggū yāzhǎng	香菇鸭掌	*duck's foot with mushroom*

Beef and lamb

niúròu	牛肉	*beef*
cōng bào niúròu	葱爆牛肉	*beef quick-fried with Chinese onions*
gōngbǎo niúròu	宫保牛肉	*stir-fried beef with peanuts and chilli*
yúxiāng niúròu	鱼香牛肉	*stir-fried beef in hot spicy sauce*
hóngshāo niúròu	红烧牛肉	*beef braised in brown sauce*
yángròu	羊肉	*lamb*
kǎo yángròuchuàn	烤羊肉串	*lamb kebabs*
shuàn yángròu	涮羊肉	*Mongolian hotpot*

Fish and seafood

yú	鱼	*fish*
yúpiàn	鱼片	*fish slices*
tángcù yúkuài	糖醋鱼块	*sweet and sour fish*
huáliū yúkuài	滑溜鱼块	*stir-fried fish slices with thick sauce added*
xiā	虾	*prawns*
fúróng xiārén	芙蓉虾仁	*stir-fried prawns with egg white*
yóuyú	鱿鱼	*squid*
lǐyú	鲤鱼	*carp*

qīngzhēng lǐyú	清蒸鲤鱼	*steamed carp*
hóngshāo lǐyú	红烧鲤鱼	*carp braised in brown sauce*
sānsī yúchì	三丝鱼翅	*shark's fin with shredded sea cucumber, abalone, and bamboo shoots*
gānshāo huángshàn	干烧黄鳝	*eel braised with chilli and bean sauce*

Vegetables

báicài	白菜	*cabbage*
bōcài	菠菜	*spinach*
càihuā	菜花	*cauliflower*
dòuyá	豆芽	*bean sprouts*
chǎo dòuyá	炒豆芽	*stir-fried bean sprouts*
mógu	蘑菇	*mushroom*
yùmǐ	玉米	*corn*
qiézi	茄子	*aubergine*
tǔdòu	土豆	*potato*
tǔdòutiáo	土豆条	*chips*
xīhóngshì	西红柿	*tomato*
xīhóngshì chǎo jīdàn	西红柿炒鸡蛋	*stir-fried tomato with egg*
chǎo shíshū	炒时蔬	*stir-fried seasonal vegetables*

dōngsǔn biǎndòu	冬笋扁豆	*stir-fried French beans with bamboo shoots*
sùshíjǐn	素什锦	*stir-fried assorted vegetables*
xiānmó wāndòu	鲜蘑豌豆	*stir-fried peas with mushrooms*

Specialities

bāozi	包子	*steamed dumplings with minced pork or various fillings*
chāshāobāo	叉烧包	*steamed dumplings with barbecued pork filling*
xiǎolóngbāo	小笼包	*steamed dumplings with various fillings*
dòufu	豆腐	*bean curd*
dòufugān	豆腐干	*dried bean curd*
dòufupí	豆腐皮	*dried soy bean cream*
guōbā dòufu	锅巴豆腐	*bean curd fried in batter*
xiārén dòufu	虾仁豆腐	*bean curd with prawns*
sānxiān dòufu	三鲜豆腐	*"three-fresh" bean curd (with three varied ingredients)*
mápó dòufu	麻婆豆腐	*"pock-marked woman bean curd" (bean curd with minced beef in hot spicy sauce)*
fǔzhú	腐竹	*"bean curd bamboo" (dried soy bean cream, in the shape of bamboo)*

shuǐjiǎo	水饺	*Chinese ravioli*
zhēngjiǎo	蒸饺	*steamed Chinese ravioli*
guōtiē	锅贴	*fried Chinese ravioli*
hún tun (or yúntūn or chāoshǒu)	馄饨	*small Chinese ravioli in soup*
sōnghuādàn	松花蛋	*preserved eggs*
xiànbǐng	馅饼	*savoury fritter*
yóutiáo	油条	*unsweetened doughnut sticks*

Soups

zǐcài tāng	紫菜汤	*seaweed and dried prawn soup*
sānxiān tāng	三鲜汤	*"three-fresh" soup (normally prawn, meats, and a seasonal vegetable)*
shíshū ròupiàn tāng	时蔬肉片汤	*soup with sliced pork and seasonal vegetables*
shíjǐn dōngguā tāng	什锦冬瓜汤	*wintermarrow soup*
bōcài fěnsī tāng	菠菜粉丝汤	*soup with spinach and vermicelli*
xīhóngshì jīdàn tāng	西红柿鸡蛋汤	*soup with eggs and tomato*
zhàcài ròusī tāng	榨菜肉丝汤	*soup with shredded pork pickled mustard greens*

Fruit

bōluó	菠萝	*pineapple*
guǎnggān	广柑	*Guangdong sweet orange*
hāmìguā	哈密瓜	*honeydew melon*
júzi (or mìjú)	橘子 (蜜橘)	*tangerine*
lí	梨	*pear*
lìzhī	荔枝	*lychee*
píngguǒ	苹果	*apple*
pútáo	葡萄	*grape*
xiāngjiāo	香蕉	*banana*
xīguā	西瓜	*watermelon*

Desserts

básī xiāngjiāo	拔丝香蕉	*banana fritters*
bīngqílín	冰淇淋	*ice cream*
shuǐguǒ sèlā	水果色拉	*fruit salad*
shíjǐn shuǐguǒ gēng	什锦水果羹	*fruit salad soup*
bābǎo fàn	八宝饭	*"eight-treasure" rice dessert (with eight types of fruit and nuts)*
bīngtáng yín'ěr	冰糖银耳	*silver tree-ear (edible fungus) in syrup*

Drinks

shuǐ	水	*water*
guǒzhī	果汁	*fruit juice*
chá	茶	*tea*
kāfēi	咖啡	*coffee*
niúnǎi	牛奶	*milk*
dòujiāng	豆浆	*soya milk*
qìshuǐ	汽水	*aerated water*
báijiǔ	白酒	*baijiu* (a clear spirit)
píjiǔ	啤酒	*beer*
pútáojiǔ	葡萄酒	*wine*

Dictionary

English to Chinese

This dictionary contains the vocabulary from *15-Minute Chinese*, together with many other high-frequency words. You can also find additional terms for food and drink in the Menu Guide (pp.128–137).

In Chinese, the plural of nouns is normally the same as the singular. Chinese descriptive words, or adjectives, may have different endings depending on how they are used and are also often preceded by hen (*"very"*). Verbs have no tenses and don't generally change according to who or what is the subject; but there are some characters that can be added to indicate a particular time or mood—see p.112.

A

a (one) yī gè
accident shìgù
accountant kuàijìshī
ache téng
actor yǎnyuán
adaptor (plug) zhuǎnjiē chātóu
address dìzhǐ
admission: admission charge ménpiào fèi
  admission ticket ménpiào
after yǐhòu
afternoon xiàwǔ
again zài
agenda huìyì rìchéng
air conditioning kōngtiáo
air mail hángkōng yóujiàn
airport jīchǎng, fēijīchǎng
alarm clock nàozhōng
alcohol jiǔjīng
all suǒyǒu
  all the streets suǒyǒu de jiēdào
  that's all, thanks hǎo le, xièxie
allergic guòmǐn
almost chàbuduō
alone dāndú
already yǐjīng

also yě
always zǒngshì
am: I am wǒ shì
America Měiguó
American (person) Měiguórén
and hé
animal dòngwù
another (different) lìng yī gè
  (further) yòu yī gè
anniversary jìniànrì
answering machine dálùjī
antibiotics kàngshēngsù
antique shop gǔdǒngdiàn
antiseptic fángfǔjì
anything: Anything else? Háiyào qítā shípǐn ma?
apartment gōngyù, dānyuán
apple píngguǒ
appointment book rìjì
April sìyuè
architecture (study) jiànzhùxué
are: you are nǐ shì
  we are wǒmen shì
  they are tāmen shì
arm shǒubì, gēbo
arrival dàodá
arrive dàodá
art yìshù

ashtray yānhuīgāng
asleep: he's asleep tā shuìzhao le
ask wèn
asthma xiàochuǎnbìng
at zài
at the café zài kāfēi guǎn
attic gélóu
attractive mírén de
August bāyuè
aunt (maternal) yímā (paternal) gūmā
Australia Àodàlìyà
Australian (adj) Àodàlìyà
autumn qiū
awful zāotòu le

B

baby yīng'ér
baby wipes yīng'ér shīzhǐjīn
back (body) bèi
backpack bēibāo
back street hòujiē
bad huài
bag (for purchases, etc.) sùliàodài
baggage xíngli
baker miànbāo lèi, miànbāo diàn
balcony yángtái

ball qiú

bamboo zhúzi

bamboo shoots zhúsǔn

banana xiāngjiāo

band (music) yuèduì

bandage bēngdài

bank yínháng

banknote zhǐbì

bar jiǔbā

barber lǐfàdiàn

baseball bàngqiú

basketball lánqiú

bath yùgāng, xǐzǎo

bathroom wèishēngjiān, xǐzǎojiān

battery diànchí

beach hǎitān

beans dòu

beard luòsāi-húzi

beautiful měilì,hǎokàn

beauty products huàzhuāngpǐn

because yīnwéi

bed chuáng

bed runner chuángqí

bedroom wòshì

bedside table chuángtóuguì

bedspread chuángdān

beef niúròu

beer píjiǔ

before (zài)...yǐqián

begin kāishǐ

behind (zài)... hòumiàn

bell zhōng

(for door, school) líng

below (zài)...xiàmiàn

belt (clothing) yāodài

best: the best zuì hǎo

better gèng hǎo

between (zài)...zhījiān

bicycle zìxíngchē

big dà

bikini bǐjīní

hill zhàngdān

bird niǎo

birthday shēngrì

Happy birthday! Shēngrì kuàilè!

biscuit bǐnggān

bite yǎo

bitter (taste) kǔ

black hēi

blanket máotǎn, tǎnzi

blind xiā

blinds bǎiyèchuāng

blocked (road, drain) dǔzhù le

blond (adj) jīnhuángsè

blood test yànxiě

blouse nǚ chènshān

blue lán

boarding pass dēngjīpái

boat chuán

body shēntǐ

boiled zhǔ

boiled rice mǐfàn

bonnet (of car) fādòngjīgài

book (noun) shū

book (verb) dìng

bookshop shūdiàn, túshū lèi

boot xuēzi

(car) hòucāng

border (of country) biānjiè

boring méi jìng

boss lǎobǎn

both liǎng gè dōu

bottle píngzi

bottle opener kāipíngqì

bowl wǎn

box hézi

boxer quánjīshǒu

boy nánhái

boyfriend nán péngyǒu

bra xiōngzhào

bracelet shǒuzhuó

branch (of company) fēnzhī jīgòu

brandy báilándì

bread miànbāo

breakfast zǎocān

bridge (over river, etc.) dàqiáo

briefcase gōngwénbāo

bring dài

Britain Yīngguó

British (adj)Yīngguó

broken (out of order) huài le

(leg) duàn le

brooch xiōngzhēn

brother (older) gēge (younger)dìdi

brown zōngsè

bruise shānghén

brush shuāzi

Buddha Fó

budget yùsuàn

building lóufáng

bulb (light) dēngpào

bumper bǎoxiǎngàng

bungalow píngfáng

burglar páshǒu, qièzéi

Burma Miǎndiàn

burn (noun) shāoshāng

bus gōnggòng qìchē

business shēngyì

business card míngpiàn

business person shāngrén

bus station gōnggòng qìchē zǒngzhàn

bus stop chēzhàn

busy (street) rènao (person) hěn máng (phone line) zhànxiàn

but dànshì

butcher ròu lèi, ròudiàn

butter huángyóu

button niǔkòu

buy mǎi

by zuò

by train/car zuò huǒchē/zuò qìchē

C

cabinet (kitchen) guìchú

cable TV yǒuxiàn diànshì

café kāfēi tīng,cháguǎn

cake dàngāo-

cake shop gāodiǎn lèi

calculator jìsuànqì

call: What is this called? Zhè jiào shénme?

calligraphy shūfǎ

camera zhàoxiàngjī

can (tin) guàntou

can: Can I ...? Wǒ kěyǐ...ma?
Can you ...? Nǐ néng bù néng ...?
he can't ... tā bù néng...

can opener guàntou qǐzi

Canada Jiānádà

candle làzhú

canopy yǔlián

Cantonese (adj) Guǎngdōng (language) Guǎngdōnghuà

cap màozi

car qìchē, chē
car park tíngchēchǎng

card (business) míngpiàn

cards (playing) pūkè

careful: Be careful! Xiǎoxīn!

carpenter mùjiàng

carpet dìtǎn

car seat (for a baby) yīng'ér qìchē ānquán zuòyǐ

cash (money) xiànjīn

cash point zìdòng tíkuǎnjī

cassette cídài

cat māo

CD-drive guāngqū

ceiling tiānhuābǎn

centre (of town) zhōngxīn

chair yǐzi
swivel chair zuòyǐ

change (verb: money) huànqián, duìhuàn
(noun: money) língqián
(verb: clothes, trains) huàn

charger chōngdiànqì

check-in bànlǐ dēngjī shǒuxù

cheque zhīpiào

chequebook zhīpiàoběn

cheque card zhīpiàokǎ

cheese nǎilào

chef chúshī

chemist (pharmacy) yàofáng

chess xiàngqí

chest (body) xiōng

chewing gum kǒuxiāngtáng

chicken jī
(meat) jīròu

child, children háizi

children's ward xiǎo'ér bìngfáng

chilli powder làjiāofěn

China Zhōngguó

China tea Zhōngguó chá

Chinese (adj) Zhōngguó
(person) Zhōngguórén
(language) Hànyǔ

the Chinese Zhōngguó rénmín

Chinese New Year Zhōngguó Chūn Jié

Chinese-style zhōngshì

chips zhá tǔdòutiáo

chocolate qiǎokèlì

chopsticks kuàizi

church jiàotáng

cigar xuějiā

cigarette xiāngyān

cinema diànyǐngyuàn

city chéngshì

clean (adj) gānjìng

cleaner (person) qīngjiégōng

clever cōngmíng

clock zhōng

close (verb) guān

close: to be close (near) jìn

closed guān le, xiūxi

clothes yīfu

clothes peg yīfu jiàzi

coach (train) chēxiāng
sleeper coach yìngwò chēxiāng
ordinary coach pǔtōng chēxiāng

coast hǎibīn

coat (overcoat) dàyī
(jacket) wàiyī

coat hanger yījià

cockroach zhāngláng

coconut yēzi

coconut milk yēzi zhī

coffee kāfēi

coins yìngbì

cold (illness) gǎnmào
(temperature) lěng

collect/reverse charge call duìfāng fùkuǎn

colour yánsè

comb shūzi

come lái
Come in! Qǐng jìn!
please come! Lái ba!

Communist Party gòngchǎndǎng

Communist Party member gòngchǎndǎngyuán

company (firm) gōngsī

complicated fùzá

computer diànnǎo, jìsuànjī

computer repair shop diànnǎo xiūlǐdiàn

concert yīnyuèhuì

condom bìyùntào

conference yántǎohuì

consulate lǐnshìguǎn

contact lenses yǐnxíng yǎnjìng

contract (noun) hétong

cool (day, weather) liángkuai

cook (chef) chúshī

corner (street) jiējiǎo

corridor zǒuláng

cost jiàqián
What does it cost? Zhè yào duōshao qián?

cot diàochuáng, yīng'ér chuáng

cotton miánhua

cotton wool yàomián

cough késou

country (nation) guójiā

cow niú

crab pángxiè

cramp jìngluán

cream (to eat) nǎiyóu

credit card xìnyòngkǎ

crime fànzuì

crisps zhá tǔdòupiàn

crocodile èyú

crossing (street) bānmǎxiàn

crowd rénqún

crowded yōngjǐ

Cultural Revolution Wénhuàdàgémìng

cup bēizi
  a cup of coffee yì bēi kāfēi

curry gālí

curtains chuānglián

customs hǎiguān

cut qiē

cyclist qí zìxíngchē de rén

D

dairy (products) rǔzhìpǐn

dangerous wēixiǎn

dark hēi'àn

daughter nǚ'ér

day tiān

dead sǐ le

deaf ěr lóng

December shí'èryuè

deep shēn

delayed wǎndiǎn

delicatessen shúshí lèi

delicious hǎochī

delivery jiāofù

dentist yáyī, yákē yīshēng

deodorant chúchòujì

department (of company) bù

department store bǎihuò shāngdiàn, bǎihuò dàlóu

departure(s) chūfā

designer shèjìshī

desk bàngōngzhuō

desserts tiándiǎn

develop (film) chōngxǐ

diabetes tángniàobìng

diarrhoea lādùzi

diary rìzhì

dictionary zìdiǎn

die sǐ

different bùtóng

difficult kùnnán

dining room cāntīng

dinner wǎncān

dinner party wǎnyàn

dirty zāng

disabled cánfèi

disco dísíkē

dish washer xǐwǎnjī

disposable nappies niàobùshī

divorced líhūn le

do zuò

doctor yīshēng

document wénjiàn

dog gǒu

dollar měiyuán

Don't! Bùyào!

door mén
  (vehicle) chēmén

double room shuāngrénfáng

drawer chōutì

down: down there xiàmiàn

dress (woman's) liányīqún

dressing gown chènyī

drink (verb) hē

drinking water yǐnyòngshuǐ

drinks (catagory) yǐnliào

driving licence jiàzhào

drops (medicinal) yàoshuǐ

drunk hēzuì le

dry gān

dry cleaner's gānxǐdiàn

dynasty cháodài
  the Ming/Ch'ing Dynasty Míngcháo/ Qīngcháo

E

each měi yì gè

ear ěrduo

earphones ěrjī

early zǎo

earring ěrhuán

east dōng

easy róngyì

eat chī

egg jīdàn

egg noodles jīdàn miàn

eight bā, bā gè

either ... or ... bù shì ... jiùshì...

elastic yǒu tánxìng de

elbow zhǒu

electrician diàngōng

electricity diàn, gōngdiàn

electronics store diànqì shāngdiàn

else: something else bié de dōngxi
  Anything else? Háiyào qítā dōngxi ma?
  somewhere else bié de dìfang

email diànzǐ yóujiàn

email address diànzǐ yóuzhǐ

embarrassing gāngà

embassy dàshǐguǎn

emergency jǐnjí qíngkuàng

emergency ward jízhěnshì

emperor huángdì

empty kōng

end (noun) mòduān

engaged (to be married) dìnghūn le

engine fādòngjī

engineer gōngchéngshī

engineering (study) gōngkè

England Yīngguó

English (person) Yīngguórén
  (language) yīngyǔ

enough gòu le

entrance rùkǒu, rùchǎng

envelope xìnfēng

epilepsy diānxiánzhèng

eraser xiàngpí

estimate gūsuàn

evening wǎnshang
every měi yī gè
  every day měi tiān
  every week měi xīngqī
everyone měi yī gè rén
everything měi jiàn shìqíng
everywhere měi gè dìfāng
excellent hǎojí le
exchange (goods) gēnghuàn
exchange rate huìlǜ
excuse me (to get attention) qǐng wèn, láojià
  (Pardon?) Qǐng zài shuō yī biàn, hǎo ma?
exhibition zhǎnshìhuì
exit chūkǒu
expensive guì
eye yǎn, yǎnjīng
eyebrow méi
eye-witness mùjīzhě

F

face liǎn
factory gōngchǎng
family jiātíng
fan (mechanical) fēngshàn
  (hand-held) shànzi
far (away) yuǎn
fare chēpiào
farmer nóngmín
fashion shíyàng
fast kuài
fat (person) pàng
father fùqin
  my father bàba
fax chuánzhēn
fax machine chuánzhēnjī
February èryuè
feel gǎnjué
  I feel hot. Wǒ juéde rè.
ferry dùchuán
fever fāshāo
few: a few yīxiē

fiance(e) wèihūn fū/qī
field tiándì
  (rice, paddy) dàotián
figures (e.g. sales) zǒngjì
film (camera) jiāojuǎn
  (movie) diànyǐng
find zhǎo
finger shǒuzhǐtou
fire huǒ
  There's a fire!
  Zháohuǒ la!
fire extinguisher mièhuǒqì
first dì-yī
fish yú
fisherman yúmín
fishmonger yú lèi
fishing diàoyú
fishing boat yúchuán
fizzy qǐpào de
five wǔ, wǔ gè
flag qízi
flash (for camera) shǎnguāngdēng
flat (adj) píngtǎn
flat tyre chētāi méiqì le
flavour wèidào
flea tiàozǎo
flight hángbān
floor (of room) dìbǎn
  (storey) lóu
florist huāhuìdiàn
flower huā, huār
fly (insect) cāngying
fly (verb) fēi
flyover lìjiāoqiáo
folk music mínjiān yīnyuè
fond: I'm fond of wǒ xǐhuān
food shíwù
food poisoning shíwù zhòngdú
foot jiǎo
foot treatment (spa) zúliáo
football zúqiú
for: for her wèi tā

  that's for me zhè shì gěi wǒ de
  a bus for ... qù ... de gōnggòng qìchē
forbidden jìnzhǐ
Forbidden City Gùgōng
foreigner wàiguó rén
forest sēnlín
fork chāzi
four sì, sì gè
fountain pēnquán
fracture gǔzhé
free (of charge) miǎnfèi
  to be free (available) yǒu kòng
freezer bīngguì
Friday xīngqīwǔ
fridge bīngxiāng
fried chǎo
fried noodles chǎomiàn
fried rice chǎofàn
friend péngyǒu
friendly yǒuhǎo
friendship store yǒuyí shāngdiàn
from: from Beijing to Shanghai cóng Běijīng dào Shànghǎi
front qiánmiàn
frozen foods lěngdòng shípǐn
fruit shuǐguǒ
ruit juice guǒzhī
fry (deep fry) zhá
  (stir fry) chǎo
full mǎn
  I'm full wǒ bǎo le
funny (strange) qíguài
  (amusing) yǒu yìsi
furniture jiājù

G

garden huāyuán
garlic dàsuàn
gate (airport, etc.) dēngjīkǒu
get (obtain) dédào
get (fetch) qǔ
  (train, bus, etc) zuòchē

get:Have you got ...?Nǐ yǒu...ma?

get in (to car) shàngchē

(arrive) dàodá

get up (in morning) qǐchuáng

gift lǐwù

ginger shēngjiāng

girl nǚhái

girlfriend nǚ péngyǒu

give gěi

glad gāoxìng

glass (for drinking) jiǔbēi, bēizi

(material) bōli

glasses (spectacles) yǎnjìng

wearing glasses dài yǎnjìng

glue jiāoshuǐ

go qù

gold huángjīn

golf/golfer gāo'ěrfū

golf course gāo'ěrfū qiúchǎng

good hǎo

good morning zǎoshang hǎo

good evening wǎnshang hǎo

good night wǎn'ān

goodbye zàijiàn

government zhèngfǔ

granddaughter (son's daughter) sūnnǚ

(daughter's daughter) wàisūnnǚ

grandfather (paternal) yéye

(maternal) wàigōng

grandmother (paternal) nǎinai

(maternal) wàipó

grandson (son's son) sūnzi

(daughter's son) wài sūnzi

grapes pútáo

grass cǎo

great: that's great! Hǎojí le! Nà tài hǎo le!

Great Britain

Dàbùlièdiān

Great Wall Chángchéng

green lǜ

greengrocer shūcài lèi

green Chinese onion dàcōng

green tea lǜchá

grey huīsè

grilled shāo

ground floor yī lóu

guarantee bǎoxiūzhèng

guest kèrén

guide dǎoyóu

guidebook dǎoyóu cè

guided tour tuántǐ cānguān

gun (pistol) shǒuqiāng

(rifle) qiāng

gutter (of house) yǔshuǐcáo

H

hair tóufa

hair dryer diànchuīfēng

haircut lǐfà

hairdresser měifàdiàn

half bàn

half past one yī diǎn bàn

ham huǒtuǐ

hamburger hànbǎobāo

hammer chuízi

hand shǒu

hand towel máojīn

handbag shǒutíbāo

handkerchief shǒujuàn

handle (noun) bǎshou

handsome yīngjùn

handyman xiūlǐgōng

happen fāshēng

happy kuàilè

harbour gǎngkǒu

hard (material) yìng

(difficult) nán

hard drive yìngpán

hat màozi

hate: I hate ... wǒ zuì bù xǐhuān

have yǒu

Do you have ...?Nǐ yǒu...ma?

I don't have ... Wǒ méiyǒu...

hay fever huāfěnrè

he tā

head tóu

head office zǒngbù

headache tóu téng

headlights qiándēng

hear tīngjiàn

hearing aid zhùtīngqì

heart xīnzàng

heart condition xīnzàngbìng

heat(ing) gōngnuǎn

heavy zhòng

heel (shoe) xiégēn

(foot) jiǎogēn

hello nǐhǎo

(on the phone) wèi

help (verb) bāngzhù

help! Jiùmìng!

hepatitis gānyán

her (possessive) tā de

(object) tā

herbs (cooking) zuòliào

(medicine) cǎoyào

here zhèlǐ, zhèr

here you are gěi nǐ

hers tā de

Hi! Nǐ hǎo!

high gāo

hill xiǎoshān

him tā

his tā de

HIV positive àizībìng yángxìng

hobby àihào

holiday jiàqī

on holiday dùjià

(public) jiérì

home jiā

homosexual tóngxìngliàn

Hong Kong Xiānggǎng

horrible kěpà

horse mǎ

hospital yīyuàn

host dōngdàozhǔ

hot rè
  (to taste) là
hot spa wēnquán dùjià
hotel (superior, for
  foreigners) jiǔdiàn
  (small) lǚguǎn
hour xiǎoshí
house fángzi
household products
  jiātíng yòngpǐn
How? Zěnme?
*How long?: How long
  does it take?*
  Xūyào duōjiǔ?
How much? Duōshao?
  (money) Duōshao
  qián?
hundred bǎi
hungry: I'm hungry.
  Wǒ è le.
hurry: I'm in a hurry.
  Wǒ méi shíjiān.
hurt téng
husband zhàngfu

I

I wǒ
ice bīng
ice cream bīngqílín
if rúguǒ
ill shēngbìng le
immediately mǎshàng
impossible bú kěnéng
in zài
  in English yòng
  yīngyǔ
India Yìndù
indigestion
  xiāohuàbùliáng
inexpensive piányi
inhaler (for asthma, etc)
  xīrùqì
infection gǎnrǎn
information xìnxī,
  xiāoxī
information desk
  wènxùnchù
insect repellent
  qūchóngjì
insurance bǎoxiǎn

interesting yǒu yìsi
internet Yīntèwǎng
internet café wǎngbā
interpret zuò fānyì
invitation yāoqǐng
invoice fāpiào
Ireland Ài'ěrlán
iron (for clothes)
  yùndǒu
is shì
  he/she/it is tā shì
island dǎo
it tā
  it's expensive guì

J

jack (for car)
  qiānjīndǐng
jacket jiākèshān, wàitào
jade yù
January yīyuè
Japan Rìběn
jasmine tea huāchá
jeans niúzǎikù
jeweller zhūbǎodiàn
jewellery shǒushì
job gōngzuò
jug guàn
July qīyuè
June liùyuè
junk (boat) fānchuán
just (only) jǐnjǐn
  just one jiù yī gè

K

karaoke kǎlā-OK
  karaoke bar kǎlā-OK
  tīng
key yàoshi
keyboard jiànpán
kick (verb) tī
kilo gōngjīn
kilometre gōnglǐ
kitchen chúfáng
knee xī
knife dāo
know: I don't know wǒ bù
  zhīdào

Korea: North Korea Běi
  Cháoxiǎn
  South Korea Nán
  Cháoxiǎn, Hánguó

L

lady nǚshì
lake hú
lamp dēng, diàndēng
lane xiǎoxiàng
Laos Lǎowō
laptop (computer)
  bǐjìběn diànnǎo
large dà
last (previous) shàng yī
  gè
  last month
  shànggeyuè
  (final) zuìhòu
last name xìng
last year qùnián
late (at night) wǎn
  (behind schedule), wǎn
  diǎn le, chí
later yǐhòu
law (study) fǎlǜ
lawyer lǜshī
lecture (university) jiǎngzuò
lecture theatre jiàoshì
lecturer (university)
  dàxué jiǎngshī
left (not right) zuǒ
  on the left zài zuǒbiān
leg tuǐ
leisure time xiūxián
  yúlè
lemon níngméng
lemonade níngméng
  qìshuǐ
letter (in post) xìnjiàn
letter box xìnxiāng
lettuce wōjù, shēngcài
library túshūguǎn
lie down tǎng
life shēnghuó
lift (elevator) diàntī
  Could you give me a lift?
  Nǐ néng bù néng ràng
  wǒ dā gè chē?

light (noun) dēng
  Have you got a light? Jiè gè huǒ xíng ma?
  (not heavy) qīng
light bulb dēngpào
lighter dǎhuǒjī
like: I'd like qǐng gěi wǒ / wǒ xiǎng...
  I like wǒ xǐhuān
  the one like that xiàng nèige yīyàng
line (phone) xiàn
  outside line wàixiàn
  (transport route) lù
lipstick kǒuhóng
literature (study) wénkē
litre shēng
little xiǎo
  just a little jiù yīdiǎndiǎn
liver gān
living room kètīng
lobster lóngxiā
long cháng
lose: I've lost my ... wǒ ...diū le
lost property shīwù zhāolǐngchù
lot: a lot xǔduō
  a lot of money xǔduō qián
loud dàshēng de
love: I love you wǒ ài nǐ
  I'd love to come wǒ yīdìng lái
lovely (person) kě'ài
  (thing) hěn hǎo
low dī
luck yùnqì
  good luck! Zhù nǐ hǎoyùn!
luggage xíngli
luggage storage xíngli jìcúnchù
lunch wǔcān

M

make zuò
make-up huàzhuāngpǐn
main courses zhǔshí
man nánrén, nánshì
manager jīnglǐ
Mandarin pǔtōnghuà
map dìtú
March sānyuè
market shìchǎng
married: I'm married wǒ jiéhūn le
martial arts wǔshù
massage ànmó
matches huǒchái
material (cloth) bù
matter: What's the matter? (asking about illness) Nǎli bù shūfu?
May wǔyuè
me wǒ
  it's for me zhè shì gěi wǒ de
meat ròu
mechanic jīxièshī
medicine (medication) yào
medicine (study) yīkē
meet (someone) jiàn
meeting huìyì
melon guā
memory (computer) nèicún
men's toilets nán cèsuǒ
menu càidān
  set menu tàocān
metre mǐ
middle: in the middle zài zhōngjiān
middle-aged zhōngnián
midnight: at midnight bànyè
mile yīnglǐ
milk niúnǎi
million bǎiwàn
mine: it's mine shì wǒ de
mineral water kuàngquánshuǐ
minute fēn
mirror jìngzi
Miss xiǎojiě
mistake cuòwù
mobile phone shǒujī
modem shùjùjī, tiáozhìjiětiáoqì

Monday xīngqīyī
money qián
Mongolia Měiguó
  Inner Mongolia Nèiměng
  Outer Mongolia Wàiměng
monkey hóu
month yuè
moon yuèliang
more gèng duō
  more than bǐ...duō
morning shàngwǔ, zǎoshang
mosquito wénzi
mosquito net (on door) shāmén
  (on window) shāchuāng
mother mǔqin
  my mother māma
motorbike mótuōchē
mountain shān
mountain climbing dēngshān
mouse (computer) shǔbiāo
  (animal) lǎoshǔ
moustache xiǎohúzi
mouth zuǐ, zuǐba
Mr ... ... xiānsheng
Mrs ... ... fūrén
Ms ... ... nǚshì
much duō
  much better hǎode duō
museum bówùguǎn
mushrooms mógu
music yīnyuè
must: I must wǒ bìxū
my ... wǒ de
  my name ... wǒ de míngzi...

N

name míngzi
nappies niàopiàn
narrow zhǎi
near jìn
  Is it near here? Lí zhèli jìn ma?

nearby fùjìn

necessary bìyào

neck bózi

necklace xiàngliàn

need: I need a ... wǒ xūyào..., wǒ xiǎng...

needle zhēn

Nepal Níbó'ěr

nephew zhízi

never cónglái bù

new xīn

news xīnwén

newspaper bàozhǐ

New Year xīnnián
  Happy New Year! Xīnnián hǎo!

New Zealand Xīnxīlán

next xià yī gè
  next month xià gè yuè
  next to ... zài... pángbiān

nice (person, weather) hěn hǎo
  (meal) hǎochī
  (town) hěn hǎo
  How nice! Nà tài hǎo le!

niece zhínǚ

night yè
  (stay in hotel) tiān

nine jiǔ, jiǔ gè

no bù
  no entry jìnzhǐ jìnrù
  no parking jìnzhǐ tíngchē

noisy chǎonào

noodles miàntiáo

noon: at noon zhōngwǔ

normal zhèngcháng

north běi

nose bízi

not bù
  not for me wǒ bù yào

notepad shūxiězhǐ

nothing méiyǒu shénme

November shíyīyuè

now xiànzài

number (quantity) shùzì
  (numeral) hàomǎ
  telephone number diànhuà hàomǎ

nurse hùshi

nuts jiānguǒ

O

occupied (toilets) yǒurén

o'clock ...diǎn

October shíyuè

*of...*de
  the name of the hotel lǚguǎn de míngzi

office bàngōngshì

office worker bàngōng rényuán

often jīngcháng

oil (motor)jīyóu
  (vegetable) càiyóu

ointment yàogāo

OK hǎo

old (person) lǎo
  (things) jiù

on zài...shàngmiàn
  on the roof zài fángdǐng
  on the beach zài hǎitān

one yī, yī gè
  that one nèi yī gè

onion yángcōng

only zhǐyǒu

open (verb) kāi
  (adj) kāi le

operating theatre shǒushùshì

operator (phone) zǒngjì

opera gējù
  Chinese opera jīngjù

opposite duìmiàn
  opposite the ... zài...duìmiàn

optician yǎnjìngdiàn

or huòzhě

orange (fruit) gānjú
  (colour) júhuángsè

orange juice chéngzhī

order (for goods, etc) dìnggòu, dìngdān

other: the other lìng yī gè

other (ones) qítā

our(s) wǒmen de

out: she's out tā bù zài

outside wàimiàn

over: over there zài nàli

own: on my own zìjǐ

oyster háo

P

pack (of cigarettes, etc) bāo

package bāoguǒ

paddy field dàotián

page yè

pagoda bǎotǎ

pain téng

painting (hobby) huàhuà

pair yī shuāng

panda xióngmāo

paper zhǐ

parasol yángsǎn

pardon? Nǐ shuō shénme?

parcel yóubāo

parents fùmǔ

park (noun) gōngyuán
  (verb) tíngchē

parking space chēkù

party (celebration) wǎnhuì
  (group) tuántǐ

pass (mountain) guānkǒu

passenger chéngkè

passport hùzhào

passport control biānfáng jiǎnchá

password mìmǎ

patient (hospital, doctor, etc) bìngrén

path xiǎolù

pavement rénxíngdào

pavilion tíngzi

pay fùqián
  Can I pay, please? Wǒ kěyǐ fùqián ma?

payment fùkuǎn

pen bǐ

pencil qiānbǐ

penicillin qīngméisù

penknife xiǎodāo

people rén

pepper (spice) hújiāo
(red/green) shìzijiāo
per: ... per cent bǎifēn
zhī...
perfume xiāngshuǐ
perhaps kěnéng
perm tàng,tàngfà
person rén
petrol qìyóu, shíyóu
petrol station
jiāyóuzhàn
pharmacy yàofáng
phonecard diànhuàkǎ
photocopy fùjìn
photocopier fùyìnjī
photograph (noun)
zhàopiàn
(verb) zhàoxiàng
photographer
shèyǐngshī
phrase book duìhuà
shǒucè
physics (study) wùlǐxué
pickpocket páshǒu
picture túpiàn
piece piàn
a piece of ...
yī piàn...
pig zhū
pillow zhěntou
pin biézhēn
pineapple bōluó
pink fěnhóng
pipe (smoking) yāndǒu
(water) guǎnzi
place dìfāng
plane fēijī
plant zhíwù
plaster (sticking)
chuāngkětiē
plastic bag sùliàodài
plate cāndié, pánzi
platform zhàntái
play (in theatre) huàjù
play (verb)
(sports, etc) dǎ
(instrument) lā
please: yes, please
kěyǐ, qǐng
Please? Hǎo ma?
pleased gāoxìng
plug (electric)chātóu

plumber guǎndàogōng
pocket yīdài
poisonous yǒudú de
police jǐngchá
police officer jǐngguān
police report jǐngfāng
bàogào
police station
jǐngchájú
polite yǒu lǐmào
politics zhèngzhì
pond chítáng
pool shuǐchí
poor (not rich) qióng
pop music liúxíng
yīnyuè
pork zhūròu
porter (hotel) ménfáng
(station, etc) bānyùn
gōngrén
possible kěnéng
post yóujiàn
post office yóujú
postbox yóuxiāng
postcard míngxìnpiàn
postman yóudìyuán
poster zhāotiē
potato tǔdòu
pound (money)
yīngbàng
prawn dāixiā
pregnant huáiyùn
present (gift) lǐwù
pretty piàoliang
price jiàgé
printer (machine)
dǎyìnjī
problem wèntí
professor jiàoshòu
profits lìrùn
pronounce fāyīn
pull lā
purse qiánbāo
push tuī
pyjamas shuìyī

Q

quarter yīkè
quarter past one

yī diǎn yīkè
quarter to two
yī diǎn sānkè
question wèntí
queue (noun) duì
quick kuài
quiet (place, hotel, etc)
ānjìng
quite: quite a lot
xiāngdāng duō

R

rabbit tù
radiator sànrèqì
radio shōuyīnjī
railway tiělù
rain yǔ
it's raining xiàyǔ le
rash (on body) zhěnzi
rat lǎoshǔ
raw shēngchī
razor tìdāo
razor blades tìhú
dāopiàn
read dú
reading (pastime)
dúshū
ready zhǔnbèi hǎo
ready meals jíshí shípǐn
receipt fāpiào, shōujù
reception (party, etc)
jiēdàishì
(hotel, etc) jiēdàichù
record (music)
chàngpiàn
red hóng
red tea hóngchá
refrigerator bīngxiāng
religion zōngjiào
rent (for room, etc)
fángzū
(verb) zū
for rent chūzū
repair xiūlǐ
report (noun)
bàogàoshū
request (noun) qǐngqiú
reservation yùdìng
restaurant cānguǎn

return (come back)
fǎnhuí
(give back) huán

return ticket
wǎnfǎn piào

rice (cooked) mǐfàn
(uncooked) mǐ

rice bowl fànwǎn

rice cooker
diànfànbāo

rice field dàotián

rich (person) hěn
yǒuqián

right (not left) yòu
on the right zài
yòubiān
(correct) duì

ring (on finger) jièzhi

river hé

road lù

roasted kǎo

rocks yánshí

roof wūdǐng, fángdǐng

room (hotel, house)
fángjiān
(space) kōngjiān

room service sòngcān
fúwù

rope shéngzi

round (adj) yuán de

rubber (material)
xiàngjiāo

rubber band
sōngjǐndài

rubbish lājī

ruins fèixū

run pǎo

Russia Éluósī

S

sad shāngxīn

safe (not in danger)
píng'ān
(not dangerous)
ānquán

safety pin biézhēn

salad sèlā

sales (company)
xiāoshòu

salt yán

same yīyàng

the same again, please
zàilái yī gè

sand shā

sandals liángxié

sandwich sānmíngzhì

sanitary towels
wèishēngjīn

satellite TV
wèixīng diànshì

Saturday xīngqīliù

sauce jiàng

sausage xiāngcháng

*say: How do you say ... in
Chinese?*
Yòng Hànyǔ zěnme
shuō...?

school xuéxiào

science (study) lǐkē

scissors jiǎndāo

Scotland Sūgélán

screen píngmù

screwdriver luósīdāo

sea hǎi

seafood hǎixiān

seat zuòwèi
take a seat zuò

seat belt ānquándài

second (in series) dì-èr
(of time) miǎo

secretary mìshū

section (of shop) dìfāng

see kànjiàn
I see! Shì zhèyang!

self-employed gètǐhù

sell mài

seminar zuòtánhuì

separately (pay) fēnkāi
fù

September jiǔyuè

serious (illness)
yánzhòng

sesame oil máyóu

set (theatre) bùjǐng

seven qī, qī gè

shade: in the shade
zài yīnliáng chù

shampoo xǐfàjīng

shave guā húzi

shaving cream
tìxūgāo

she tā

sheep yáng

sheet (for bed)
chuángdān

ship chuán

shirt chènshān

shoelaces xiédài

shoes xiézi

shoeshop xiédiàn

shop shāngdiàn

shopkeeper diànzhǔ

shopping (activity)
gòuwù

shopping trolley
shǒutuīchē

short ǎi
(time) duǎn

shorts duǎnkù

shoulder jiānbǎng

shower (in bathroom)
línyù

shower gel yùyè

shrimp xiā

shut guān

shutter bǎiyèchuāng

Siberia Xībólìyà

siblings xiōngdì

side street xiǎojiē

sight: the sights of...
fēngjǐng

sightseeing guānguāng

signature qiānmíng

silk sīchóu

Silk Road sīchóu zhī lù

silver yín

sing chànggē

Singapore Xīnjiāpō

single: I'm single wǒ shì
dānshēn

single room dānrén fáng

single ticket
dānchéngpiào

sink shuǐchí

sister (older) jiějie
(younger) mèimei

sit zuò

six liù, liù gè

skirt qúnzi

sky tiānkōng

sleep shuìjiào

sleeper coach yìngwò
chēxiāng

sleeve xiùzi

slippers tuōxié

slow(ly) màn

small xiǎo

smell (have bad smell) nánwén de qìwèi

smile (verb) xiào

smoke (noun) yān
 Do you smoke? Nǐ xīyān ma?

snacks xiǎochī

snake shé

so: so good zhēn hǎo
 not so much bùyào nàme duō

soap féizào

socks wàzi

socializing shèjiāo

sofa shāfā

soft (material, etc) ruǎn

soft drink (ruan) yǐnliào

soil (earth) tǔ

sole (of shoes) xiédǐ

somebody yǒurén

something yǒuxiē dōngxi

sometimes yǒushí

somewhere mǒuchù

son érzi

song gē

soon bùjiǔ

sorry duìbuqǐ
 Sorry? Nǐ shuō shénme?

soup tāng

south nán

souvenir jìniànpǐn

soy sauce jiàngyóu

speak jiǎng

spider zhīzhū

spoon tiáogēng, sháozi

sport yùndòng

spring (season) chūn

spring onion xiǎocōng

square guǎngchǎng

stage (theatre) wǔtái

stairs lóutī

stamp (for letter) yóupiào

stapler dìngshūjī

start (noun) kāishǐ

starters tóupán

statement (e.g. witness) zhèngcí

station (railway) huǒchē zhàn

steak niúpái

steal: My bag has been stolen.
 Wǒ de bāo bèi tōu le.
 What was stolen?
 Diūshī le shénme?

steamed zhēng

steps táijiē

sticky rice nuòmǐ

stockings chángtǒngwà

stomach fù, dùzi, wèi

stomachache wèi téng

stones shítou

stop (bus stop) chēzhàn
 stop! Tíng!
 stop here zài zhèlǐ tíng

storm bàofēngyǔ

stove lúzào

straight; it's straight ahead yīzhí cháoqián
 go straight on zhàozhí zǒu

street jiē

string xìshéng

student xuéshēng

stupid yúchǔn

sugar táng

suit (noun) xīzhuāng

suitcase xiāngzi

summer xià

Summer Palace Yíhéyuán

sun tàiyáng

sunblock (cream) fángshàirǔ

sunburnt shàihēi de

Sunday xīngqīrì

sunglasses tàiyángjìng

sunshade yángsǎn

sunstroke zhòngshǔ

suntan lotion fángshàijì

supermarket chāoshì

suppository shuānjì

sure: I'm sure wǒ quèxìn
 Are you sure? Nǐ néng kěndìng ma?

sweat (noun) hàn
 (verb) chūhàn

sweater tàoshān

sweet (adj) tián
 (confectionery) tángguǒ

sweet and sour tángcù

sweltering: it's sweltering mēnrè

swim (verb) yóuyǒng

swimming yóuyǒng

swimsuit yóuyǒngyī

swimming pool yǒngchí

swimming trunks yǒngkù

syringe zhùshèqì

syrup (medicinal) tángjiāng

T

table zhuōzi

table tennis pīngpāng

tablets yàopiàn

Taiwan Táiwān

take (transport) chéng
 (someone somewhere) dàilǐng
 (something somewhere) dài

talk (verb) shuōhuà

tall gāo

tampons miánsāi

Taoism Dàojiào

tap shuǐlóngtóu

tape (cassette) cídài
 (invisible adhesive) tòumíng jiāodài

taxi chūzūchē

taxi rank chūzūchē zhàn

tea chá
 tea with milk nǎichá

teacher lǎoshī

telegram diànbào

telephone diànhuàjī, diànhuà
 telephone card diànhuàkǎ, IP-kǎ
 telephone number

diànhuà hàomǎ

television diànshì

tell gàosù

temperature (weather)
qìwēn
(fever) fāshāo

temple miào

tent zhàngpéng

terminal (airport,
etc.) hòujīlóu

Terracotta Army
bīngmǎyǒng

terrible zhēn
zāogāo

test (hospital) huàyàn

Thailand Tàiguó

than bǐ...gèng
smaller than
bǐ...xiǎo

thank you xièxie (nǐ)

that: that woman
nèigè nǚrén
that man nèige
nánrén
What's that? Nà shì
shénme?

theatre jùchǎng, jùyuàn

their(s) tāmen de

them tāmen

theme park
zhǔtí gōngyuán

then (after that) ránhòu
(at that time) nà shí

there nàli
there is/are yǒu...
Is/are there...?
Yǒu...ma?
there isn't/aren't ...
méiyǒu...

thermos flask
rèshuǐpíng

these zhèxiē

they tāmen

thick hòu

thief páshǒu

thin (thing) báo
(person) shòu

thing dōngxi

think xiǎng

thirsty: I'm thirsty wǒ
kǒukě

this: this street zhè tiáo jiē
this one zhège
what's this? Zhè shì
shénme?

thousand qiān
ten thousand wàn

those nàxiē

three sān, sān gè

throat hóulong

through jīngguò

thunderstorm léiyǔ

Thursday xīngqīsì

Tibet Xīzàng

ticket piào
admission ticket
ménpiào
train/bus ticket
chēpiào
airline ticket jīpiào

tie (around neck)
lǐngdài

tiger hǔ

tights kùwà

time shíjiān
next time xià cì
on time zhǔndiǎn
What time is it?
Xiànzài jǐ diǎn le?

timetable shíjiānbiǎo

tip (money) xiǎofèi

tired lèi

tissues shǒuzhǐ

to dào
to England qù
Yīnggélán

toast (bread) kǎo
miànbāopiàn

today jīntiān

tofu dòufu

tofu shop dòufudiàn

together yīqǐ

toilet cèsuǒ

toilet paper
wèishēngzhǐ

tomato xīhóngshì

tomorrow míngtiān

tonic (water)
kuàngquánshuǐ

tonight jīntiān
wǎnshang

too (also) yě
(excessively) tài

tooth yá

toothache yá téng

toothbrush yáshuā

toothpaste yágāo

tour (noun) lǚxíng

tourist lǚxíngzhě

*tourist information
office* lǚyóu
fúwù zhōngxīn

towel máojīn

town chéngzhèn

traditional chuántǒng

traffic lights
hónglǜdēng

train huǒchē

transformer biànyāqì

translate fānyì

travel agent lǚxíngshè

traveller's cheque
lǚxíngzhīpiào

travelling lǚyóu

tree shù

trip (journey) lǚxíng

trolley shǒutuīchē

trousers kùzi, chángkù

true zhēn de

try (test) shìshi

T-shirt duǎnxiù
yuánlǐng hànshān

Tuesday xīngqī'èr

turn zhuǎn
turn left zuǒ zhuǎn
turn right yòu zhuǎn

two èr, liǎng gè

tweezers nièzi

tyre chētāi, lúntāi

U

umbrella yǔsǎn

uncle shūshu

under zài...xiàmiàn

underground (metro)
dìtiě

underground station
dìtiě zhàn

unfortunately kěxī

United States Měiguó

university dàxué

university lecturer
dàxué jiǎngshī

urgent jízhěn

V

vaccination yùfáng jiēzhòng
vanilla xiāngcǎo
vase huāpíng
vegetables shūcài
vegetarian sùshízhě
very hěn, fēicháng
very well (OK) hǎo ba
video games diànzǐ yóuxì
video tape lùxiàngdài
Vietnam Yuènán
view (scenery) jǐngsè
village cūnzhuāng
violin xiǎotíqín
visa qiānzhèng
visit (place) cānguān
　(people) bàifǎng
visiting hours tànwàng shíjiān
voice shēngyīn
voice mail yǔyīn yóujiàn
voltage diànyā
vomit (verb) ǒutù

W

wait děng
waiter zhāodài
waiting room (clinic) hòuzhěnshì
waitress nǚzhāodài
Wales Wēi'ěrshì
wall qiáng
　the Great Wall of China Chángchéng
wallet qiánbāo
walk, go for a walk sànbù
want: I want wǒ yào
ward (hospital) bìngfáng
warm nuǎnhuo
washing machine xǐyījī
washing powder xǐyīfěn

washing-up liquid xǐjiéjīng
wasp huángfēng
watch (wrist) shǒubiǎo
　(verb) kàn
water shuǐ
we wǒmen
weather tiānqì
web site wǎngzhàn
wedding hūnlǐ
Wednesday xīngqīsān
week xīngqī
welcome huānyíng
　you're welcome bùkèqi
well: I don't feel well wǒ gǎnjué bù shūfu
west xī
Western-style xīshì
wet shī
What? Shénme?
wheel lúnzi
　(vehicle) chēlún
wheelchair lúnyǐ
When? Shén me shíhou?
Where? Nǎr?, Nǎli?
where: Where is ...? ...zài nǎli?
which: Which one? Nǎ yī gè?
whisky wēishìjì
white bái
Who? Shéi?
　Who's calling? Nín shì shuí ya?
Why? Wèi shénme?
wide kuān
wife qīzi
wind fēng
window chuānghu
windscreen dǎngfēng bōli
wine pútáojiǔ
　wine list jiǔshuǐ dān
wing mirror hòushìjìng
winter dōng
with hé...
without méiyǒu
witness zhèngrén
woman nǚrén, nǚshì

women's toilets nǚ cèsuǒ
wood mùtou
wool yángmáo
word cí
work (noun) gōngzuò
　(verb) gōngzuò
　it's not working huài le
worktop chútái
worry: don't worry bié dānxīn
wrench bānshou
write xiě
　Could you write it down? Nǐ néng bù néng xiě yīxià?
wrong cuò

X

X-ray X-guāng

Y

Yangtze Gorges Chángjiāng Sānxiá
Yangtze River Chángjiāng
year nián
yellow huáng
Yellow River Huánghé
Yellow Sea Huánghǎi
yes shì de
yesterday zuótiān
yet: not yet háiméi ne
yoghurt suānnǎi
you nǐ
　(formal) nín
　(plural) nǐmen
young niánqīng
your(s) nǐ de
　(plural) nǐmen de

Z

zip lāliàn
zoo dòngwùyuán

The Chinese writing system

Introduction

Chinese characters evolved from pictograms. These crude drawings originally resembled the object or idea they referred to (for example, an animal or a natural feature). In this way, Chinese writing developed as a series of ideograms, or characters, and not as an alphabet. But over time the characters became more complex. In modern Chinese, a few characters still bear a discernable likeness to the object they refer to, but most have changed beyond recognition.

Unlike an alphabet, Chinese characters do not carry an immediate clue as to their pronunciation – you can't look at one as a beginner and know (or even guess) how to say it. Each character needs to be learnt individually. This may at first seem like a daunting task, and no-one would pretend it is a fast process. On the other hand, when you understand how the Chinese language combines basic concepts to produce more complex ideas, you will see that even a few basic characters can take you a long way.

The purpose of this section is to show how you can start to decipher the characters, beginning with the simplest and most common. Writing the characters is another skill and one for which you will need a specialist book showing the order and direction of the strokes making up each character.

Traditional and simplified characters

During the 1950s and 1960s, the People's Republic of China (mainland China) developed a simplified set of Chinese characters in an effort to promote literacy amongst the general population. The number of strokes in many characters was reduced and the shape simplified.

The simplified set of characters is used today in mainland China, although some other Chinese-speaking regions still use the traditional set. *15-Minute Chinese* uses simplified characters as this is the most useful set for beginners to learn.

Basic concepts

Some basic concepts and natural features are represented by a single character, and the simplest of these are the easiest characters to recognize at first.

Numbers

The basic Chinese characters representing number are easily recognized. The characters for the numbers one to five also show the significance of the number and order of the strokes (see Read it box page 14).

一　　yī *(one)*　　　　　六　　liù *(six)*

二　　èr *(two)*　　　　　七　　qī *(seven)*

三　　sān *(three)*　　　八　　bā *(eight)*

四　　sì *(four)*　　　　九　　jiǔ *(nine)*

五　　wǔ *(five)*　　　　十　　shí *(ten)*

Once you can recognize and say these characters, you can combine them to produce higher numbers:

十一　　　shíyī *(eleven – "ten one")*

十二　　　shí'èr *(twelve – "ten two")*

十九　　　shíjiǔ *(nineteen – "ten nine")*

八十　　　bāshí *(eighty – "eight ten")*

四十　　　sìshí *(forty – "four ten")*

六十五　　liùshíwǔ *(sixty-five – "six ten five")*

Add one more character and you can recognize all the months of the year:

三月   sānyuè (March – "three month")

七月   qīyuè (July – "seven month")

十一月   shíyīyuè (November – "eleven month")

And another one to tell the time:

四点   sì diǎn (four o'clock – "four point")

八点   bā diǎn (eight o'clock – "eight point")

十二点   shí'èr diǎn (twelve o'clock – "twelve point")

The same principle works with the days of the week and other numerical concepts. So with just 12 characters, you can already recognize dozens of words.

Natural features

Some of the first pictograms to develop were probably those representing natural features (e.g. *river, mountain, horse,* etc.). They are still amongst the simplest and most memorable characters, sometimes retaining a resemblance to the original concept (see *mountain, tree,* and *person,* for example).

山 shān *(mountain)*   水 shuǐ *(water)*

树 shù *(tree)*   土 tǔ *(soil)*

羊 yáng *(sheep)*   马 mǎ *(horse)*

人 rén *(person)*   鱼 yú *(fish)*

Basic grammatical words

Some characters representing basic grammatical concepts recur frequently:

我 wǒ *(I)* 你 nǐ *(you)*

他 tā *(he)* 她 tā *(she)*

是 shì *(am/are/is)* 的 de *(of/belonging to)*

们 men *(plural indicator)*

If you learn to recognize these seven basic characters, the literal nature of Chinese means that you will be able to recognize a vocabulary equivalent to over three times as many English words (*I, you, he, she, we, they, my, your, his, her, our, their, mine, yours, ours, theirs, me, him, I'm, you're, we're, she's,* etc.), for example:

我们 wǒmen *(we)* 他们 tāmen *(they)*

我的 wǒ de *(my)* 你的 nǐ de *(your)*

我们的 wǒmen de *(our)*

Other common characters

There are other commonly recurring Chinese characters that will open the door to entire vocabulary sets for you, for example:

大 dà *(big)* 小 xiǎo *(small)*

车 chē *(vehicle)* 机 jī *(machine)*

店 diàn *(shop)* 好 hǎo *(good/well)*

晚 wǎn *(late/evening)* 早 zǎo *(early/morning)*

餐 cān *(meal)* 很 hěn *(very)*

You can often find these characters in combination with others. Here are a few examples from *15-Minute Chinese*:

早餐   zǎocān *(breakfast – "early meal")*

晚餐   wǎncān *(dinner – "late meal")*

餐馆   cānguǎn *(restaurant– "meal place")*

你好   nǐhǎo *(hello – "you well")*

很好   hěn hǎo *(very good)*

早上好   zǎoshang hǎo *(good morning – "early time good")*

晚上好   wǎnshang hǎo *(good evening – "late time good")*

出租车   chūzūchē *(taxi – "hire vehicle")*

火车   huǒchē *(train – "fire vehicle")*

车票   chēpiào *(ticket – "vehicle fare")*

小胡子   xiǎohúzi *(moustache – "small beard")*

小路   xiǎolù *(path – "small road")*

小吃   xiǎochī *(snacks – "small eat")*

大学   dàxué *(university – "big school")*

鞋店 xiédiàn *(shoe shop)*

书店 shūdiàn *(bookshop)*

飞机 fēijī *(plane – "flying machine")*

复印机 fùyìnjī *(photocopier – "photocopy machine")*

Summary

Understanding the principle of how the Chinese script works will enable you to break down a string of characters representing a word or phrase. It will help you identify familiar and unfamiliar characters. For example, look at the following sentence from the first conversation in *15-Minute Chinese*:

你好，我的名字是韩红。

(Hello. My name's Han Hong.)

Because you are now familiar with some basic characters, you can identify the characters that mean "hello", "my", and "is". You can also deduce the characters for "name" (名字 mingzi) and "Han Hong" (韩红). More importantly, you will understand better the structure of the Chinese sentence (literally "you well. I-belonging to name is Han Hong").

Look back over other words and phrases in *15-Minute Chinese* and do your own detective work. You will realize that every word and phrase does not have to be learnt in isolation. The common characters with their shared sounds and meanings will help you build your Chinese vocabulary.

Useful signs

Here are some useful signs you may see around you in China.
Try to apply the principle of breaking down the combinations
into their component characters to help you to recognize
them. You will also find common road signs on pp.44–45.

rùkǒu
Entrance

出口
chūkǒu
Exit

cèsuǒ
Toilets

náncèsuǒ
Men's toilet

女厕所
nǚcèsuǒ
Women's toilet

危险
wēixiǎn
Danger

jìnzhǐ xīyān
No smoking

警察局
jǐngchájú
Police station

医院
yīyuàn
Hospital

银行
yínháng
Bank

自动提款机
zìdòng tíkuǎnjī
Cash point

邮局
yóujú
Post office

火车站
huǒchē zhàn
Train station

机场
jīchǎng
Airport

Acknowledgments

The publisher would like to thank the following for their help in the preparation of this book: Tamlyn Calitz for editorial assistance, Capel Manor College, Toyota (GB), Magnet Kitchens Kentish Town, Xerox UK, Wei Wei Zhu, Hannah Ho, Lik-Chung Li, Teresa Miao, Dave Wong, Oliver Stockdale, and Clive Moset.

Language content for Dorling Kindersley by G-AND-W PUBLISHING
Managed by **Jane Wightwick**

Picture research: **Lee Riches**
Illustration: **Hugh Schermuly and Lee Riches**

Picture credits

Key:
t=top; b=bottom; l=left, r=right; c=centre; A=above; B=below

p1 **DK Images:** *Wu Ming c; p2/3* **DK Images:** *Colin Sinclair l; p4/5* **DK Images:** *tcl; Colin Sinclair tl, Linda Whitwam tr, Howard Rice br;* **Ingram Image Library:** *tcr;* **Alamy:** *mediacolor's bcl; p6/7* **Laura Knox:** *cl; p14/15* **DK Images:** *Paul Bricknell cl;* **Ingram Image Library:** *cbl, cAr; p16/17* **Ingram Image Library:** *ctr; p18/19* **DK Images:** *David Murray tr; Andy Crawford cll; p22/23* **Alamy:** *Robert Harding Picture Library Ltd cl;* **Alamy:** *mediacolor's tcr; p24/25* **Alamy:** *Charlie Lim cl;* **DK Images:** *Wu Ming bl,* **Ingram Image Library:** *tcr; p28/29* **DK Images:** *John Bulmer tcr;* **Alamy:** *Christophe Testi cr;* **Ingram Image Library:** *bcr; p30/31* **Alamy:** *David Crausby bcl;* **DK Images:** *cl;* **Alamy:** *Ferruccio cr; p34/35* **Takehisa Yano:** *tcr;* **Alamy:** *Kevin Foy tBr;* **Alamy:** *Charlie Lim cr; p36/37* **DK Images:** *cbr; p38/39* **DK Images:** *Wu Ming bl-r;* **Alamy:** *Ulana Switucha c,* **Alamy:** *Mike Goldwater tcr,* **Alamy:** *Dbimages cr; p40/41* **Alamy:** *David Robinson/Snap2000 Images cl,* **DK Images:** *Karen Trist © Rough Guides bl,* **DK Images:** *Bryn Walls tcr, tcrB, cr, bcr* **DK Images:** *Colin Sinclair cAr* **Alamy:** *David Robinson/Snap2000 Images bcrA; p42/43* **DK Images:** *Wu Ming bl-r, cr,* **DK Images:** *Bryn Walls c, tcr, tcrB, crB* **DK Images:** *Colin Sinclair crA; p44/45 Courtesy of* **Toyota (GB):** *c; p46/47* **Toyota (GB):** *ctr;* **Ingram Image Library:** *cAr;* **DK Images:** *Bryn Walls tcl,cl,* **DK Images:** *Colin Sinclair bl,* **Images:** *Karen Trist © Rough Guides cl,* **Alamy:** *Ulana Switucha br; p48/49* **DK Images:** *cl, c, bcl, bcr, Linda Whitwam tcr, Chris Stowers clA;* **Alamy:** *JTB Photo Communications, Inc. clA; p50/51* **Takehisa Yano:** *tcr;* **DK Images:** *c,* **Alamy:** *LOOK Die Bildagentur der Fotografen GmbH cr; p52/53* **DK Images:** *Colin Sinclair cl,* **DK Images:** *bl-r;* **Alamy:** *David Crausby cAr;* **DK Images:** *Wu Ming bl-r, cbr; p54/55* **Alamy:** *Frank Herhold bcl; Jackson Smith cBl; Pat Behnke cr;* **Alamy RF:** *BananaStock cl;* **ThinkStock** *tcr;* **DK Images:** *Andy Crawford bclA; p56/57* **DK Images:** *cl, clA, tl, trl; Linda Whitwam tlB, Chris Stowers tcl;* **Alamy:** *JTB Photo Communications, Inc. clA;* **Toyota (GB):** *bl, cBr; p58/59* **Alamy RF:** *Brand X Pictures cBl; Image Source cAAl; Image Source cl;* **DK Images:** *Wu Ming bl-r, cl; p60/61* **Alamy RF:** *Image Source cBr, cr* **DK Images:** *Bryn Walls bl; Steve Gorton cAAr; Pia Tryde cAr, bcr; p62/63* **DK Images:** *Wu Ming bl-r, c; Jo Foord cr; Andy Crawford crA; Geoff Brightling crB; p64/65* **DK Images:** *c;* **Alamy:** *Arcaid bcrA;* **Alamy RF:** *Diana Ninov cAr;* **Ingram Image Library:** *tcr; p66/67* **Alamy:** *Arcaid cll;* **DK Images:** *Wu Ming bc;* **Ingram Image Library:** *bcr;* **Alamy RF:** *Image Source cr; p68/69* **DK Images:** *cBr, Wu Ming clAl, cll, clBr, cbr; Geoff Brightling bl;* **Hugh Sykes:** *clAr, cl, clBl, ctr, cAr; p70/71* **DK Images:** *Wu Ming bl-r; p72/73* **Alamy RF:** *Comstock Images tcr;* **Hugh Sykes:** *tcrB;* **Alamy:** *Belinda Lawley crA; Tina Manley/Business cr; p74/75* **Alamy RF:** *Doug Norman bl; p76/77* **DK Images:** *Wu Ming bcl, bcAll, bcAlll,cbr;* **Hugh Sykes:** *bcll, bclll, bcAl; p80/81* **Getty:** *Taxi / Rob Melnychuk bc;* **Ingram Image Library:** *cAr;* **Xerox UK Ltd:** *tcr; p82/83* **Alamy:** *jack Sullivan tcr;* **Alamy RF:** *Momentum Creative Group cAl;* **Ingram Image Library:** *cl; p84/85* **DK Images:** *bl;* **Alamy RF:** *SuperStock tr; Brand X Pictures cr;* **Ingram Image Library:** *crB; p86/87* **Getty:** *Taxi / Rob Melnychuk tc;* **DK Images:** *bcrA, Wu Ming bcrAA; p88/89* **DK Images:** *Wu Ming bl-r;* **Alamy:** *Ace Stock Limited tcr; p90/91* **DK Images:** *cl; David Jordan tcr; Stephen Oliver cr;* **Ingram Image Library:** *cBr; p92/93* **Ingram Image Library:** *cl;* **Alamy RF:** *Pixland cr;* **DK Images:** *Guy Ryecart tr; p94/95* **Alamy RF:** *ImageState Royalty Free bcr;* **DK Images:** *bl-r, cbl; p96/97* **DK Images:** *cll; p98/99* **Getty Images:** *Daisuke Morita c;* **DK Images:** *Frank Greenaway bcl; p100/101* **DK Images:** *Steve Gorton tcr; p102/103* **DK Images:** *Peter Chen bl; Andrew butler tcr; Bruce Forster tcrB; Linda Whitwam cr; Howard Rice crA; p104/105* **DK Images:** *Bob Langrish cl(5); Jane Burton bl; Max Gibbs cl(3); Frank Greenaway cl(2); Tracy Morgan c(4); Dave King cl(1); p106/107* **Getty Images:** *Daisuke Morita cr;* **DK Images:** *bcr; p110/111* **Alamy RF:** *Stockbyte cl;* **Alamy:** *Charlie Lim tcr; p112/113* **Ingram Image Library:** *bl;* **Alamy:** *Real World People tcrB;* **DK Images:** *Geoff A Howard cl; p114/115* **Alamy:** *View Stock cl; Ace Stock Limited cr,* **DK Images:** *Linda Whitwam tcr; p116/117* **DK Images:** *Wu Ming bcr;* **Alamy:** *Geoff A Howard clA; p118/119* **Alamy RF:** *Stock Image/Pixland tcr;* **DK Images:** *Courtesy of the Chinese Opera Institute, Singapore cr; p120/121* **Alamy:** *ImageState cl;* **DK Images:** *bcl; p122/123* **Alamy:** *Judith Miller / Sparkle Moore at The Girl Can't Help It cl;* **DK Images:** *Geoff A Howard cr; p124/125* **DK Images:** *Bob Langrish ctr(3); Max Gibbs cl(4); Frank Greenaway clA(2); Tracy Morgan cr(5); Dave King cll(1);* **Alamy:** *ImageState bclA;* **DK Images:** *bcl; p126/127* **DK Images:** *Wu Ming cl, cll, clll;* **Ingram Image Library:** *brAA;* **Alamy:** *David Crausby cr; p128* **DK Images:** *Neil Mersh tl.*

All other studio and location images **Mike Good**